Raising Our Voices

100 Years of Women in the WEA

Edited by Zoë Munby

Women's Education
Chris Scarlett, National Co-ordinator Women's Education
Aizlewood's Mill, Nursery Street, Sheffield S3 8GG

WE*a*

A CENTURY
OF LEARNING

1903 – 2003

Contents

Introduction

As I scan these pages, I am filled with suppressed
excitement. It is a long time since I strung so many words
together, forming a dubious whole. I have always wanted
to write and doubted my single-mindedness to continue.
But I must. I have failed in my secret longing to assemble
ideas, thoughts, poetry, whatever the inspiration might be.
It is so much easier to sew a bit, or read the paper, or bake
a cake, but the challenge to write is strong. So I turn to the
women's class and our tutor, and listen. And as we read
the passages about other women, I realise that I also have a
story to tell, however modest and ordinary, and I have
enjoyed doing this for the class.

Rosina Watson, Sevenoaks women's class, 1987.

Rosina – and many women like her – have spoken and written about their lives in WEA classes over the years. Talking with others they realise the significance of their own lives, the way their achievements and struggles echo and contrast with the lives of other women. In a health discussion group, in a literature class, or a family history group it is possible to see how our lives – our history - contribute to an understanding of a bigger picture. Since the earliest days the Workers' Educational Association (known as the WEA) has encouraged students to speak about their own experience. In a WEA class local and personal aspects of subjects are related to an over-view, or theories, that a tutor brings and students are encouraged to look at the past with fresh and critical eyes. From the first decade of the WEA we find women-only classes exploring subjects such as 'Women of the Nineteenth Century' or the 'Historical Position of Women'; by the early 1970s pioneering feminist historians were developing their research in WEA women's classes.

This publication draws on these traditions: it includes existing accounts by or about women in the WEA and new research into WEA women's lives. In addition, women involved in the WEA today have written about themselves and their friends. This is a collection of biographies and autobiographies of and by women who have been involved in our organisation. We hope that it will be read by WEA students, by people who work in adult education, by people interested in women's issues and by those who are new to all these areas. These accounts may be an accessible way to begin to explore more complex ideas about education, the business of volunteering, and the lives of women and men.

The women whose lives are recorded here were all involved with the Workers' Educational Association between the years 1903 and 2003. This organisation is a bit of an oddity. It is famous, in educational circles, for its achievements in carving a route for working class men into Oxford and Cambridge universities, yet for most of its existence it has provided, overwhelmingly, classes for women. It has been a respectable government-funded adult education organisation for ninety-six years but is frequently unknown, or unrecognised, at a local level. The story of women's involvement in the organisation has not been told. Official accounts of districts and the association as a whole have focussed on the contribution of men who have held the power and influence in the voluntary and paid management of

the organisation. This account recovers some of the women whose contributions have been ignored and offers evidence for taking seriously the involvement of women.

When the WEA was founded 100 years ago working class women had few rights: they could not vote and faced enormous barriers to employment and achieving equal status in almost all areas of life. Educational opportunities for all women were extremely limited. Girls' secondary schools existed for those whose fathers were prepared to pay and a few women's colleges provided secondary and further education. Technical colleges offered vocational training, mainly to men and boys. Some, not all, universities admitted women and by 1903 a small band had been awarded degrees, although not on equal terms with men. For the vast majority of women all this was beyond their reach. Some church and socialist organisations ran evening classes for working class people, fostering self-improvement, domestic skills and basic education. For working class women in 1903, the challenge was to overcome the sheer exhaustion of daily life and the prejudices of society if they were to take advantage of any educational opportunities.

Women's lives a century later are transformed: we participate on apparently equal terms at school, in further and higher education. Laws protect our employment rights. As mothers and wives virtually all of the legal obstacles to equality have been swept aside by successive campaigns waged by women over the preceding century. Yet life, in practice and in attitudes, remains stubbornly unequal. Men still earn more than women[1]. Men occupy more senior positions at work, even in those fields where women predominate, such as education and health. Parliament, local government, trade union leadership and the senior grades of the Civil Service are overwhelmingly male. Women still bear the brunt of child rearing and domestic work. Women may lead better lives in 2003 than they did in 1903 but men's and women's lives remain very different.

To what extent has the WEA's educational work contributed to women's altered situation? Have the women-only classes or trade union education equipped women with the tools they needed to challenge the unequal world they live in, or has adult education merely soothed the frustrations of those trapped at home or in less satisfying jobs? This publication doesn't answer those questions but it

---

[1] According to the Fawcett Society women working full-time earn 80% of what men earn and women who work part-time earn 60% of what men earn.

offers evidence. As 2003 approached women in the WEA were aware that the Centenary celebrations could well repeat the gaps and distortions of earlier histories, leaving women as a sideline to the main story. There was a need to mark women's contribution in a way that also drew on the educational traditions of women's education. Whilst a serious history of women's involvement in the WEA remains to be written – and therefore any comprehensive account of the organisation as a whole – we could begin to collect the raw material for that history. In May 2001 we launched a project which invited women from across the Association to undertake local research. They could work on their own, or as part of a class, to find out about women's involvement in the WEA. The results of this project have been diverse: some districts, individual women

and some branches have thrown their energies into producing a wealth of material. The contributions received are overwhelmingly autobiographical, biographical and oral history: at the time of writing 275 women have participated and accounts are still arriving. Everything received by the project will be deposited in the WEA's national archive at the London Metropolitan University[2]. The accounts below are only part of that rich source.

Once we had made the decision to publish these accounts, there were a further set of decisions: what to include, how much context or explanation was needed and how to organise the 'lives' so that they paint a picture which is wider than simply one woman's experience. The accounts that we received were *mainly* autobiographical: mostly written

WEA leaflet published c. 1920

[2] The archive is open to the general public, by appointment, 9.15-4.45, tel. 020 7753 3184.

between 2000 and 2002 they are almost all accounts of WEA involvement during the last sixty years. Relying solely on these contributions would have left us with a very thin picture of the first forty years of the Association so we have added to the few research contributions of the earlier period. There was a similar lack of material for the last fifteen years: women with a relatively recent involvement with the organisation have been either too busy to write, or think their story is insignificant, because it is contemporary. We have sought out accounts from a number of women who we believe are representative of women in the WEA in this period.

We also needed to make sense of individual biographical accounts, to explain how a fragment of one women's life was typical, or perhaps not typical, of WEA women. There was a need to explain some of the language and structures of the organisation (branches and districts, voluntary educational advisors and class secretaries) and how they have developed over 100 years. So threaded through the 'lives' are essays which explain some of the context of the WEA experience. We have chosen to arrange the lives around categories of involvement: students, volunteers, teachers, organisers; women working in the district office; women involved with the national association. Yet these categories are themselves problematic. A characteristic of women's involvement has been the movement between different kinds of role – they start as students and become volunteers; volunteers become district secretaries – the most senior post within districts – and in one instance here, are demoted back to an

administrative role. These role fluctuations tell us about women's lives in the wider society, as well as how the WEA has treated women and how women have made use of the WEA. In choosing how to categorise individuals, we have selected the role from which they write, the focus of their account.

The last element in the making of this book has been the 'we' who are represented in this introduction. There are several: the national Women's Education Committee has sponsored and guided the project throughout; a smaller group of four women have met periodically over two years to make detailed decisions. The views of WEA women have been canvassed when opportunities arose. One woman has acted as co-ordinator for the project and has taken on the task of compilation, writing the essays and filling the gaps. This book contains the words of many women and is the result of the understanding created by *all* the contributions received by the wider project. A group of six women have read and commented on this book in draft. By drawing on the collective approaches of women's education, and of the WEA at its best, we hope to make women's role in the organisation visible and acknowledged.

This publication has been made possible by money left in trust by Margaret James to support women's education. Her story, like many other WEA women, had not survived. The account of Annie Winner's research to 'find' Margaret James illustrates how easy it is for women's lives to disappear and how important it is to place on record these lives.

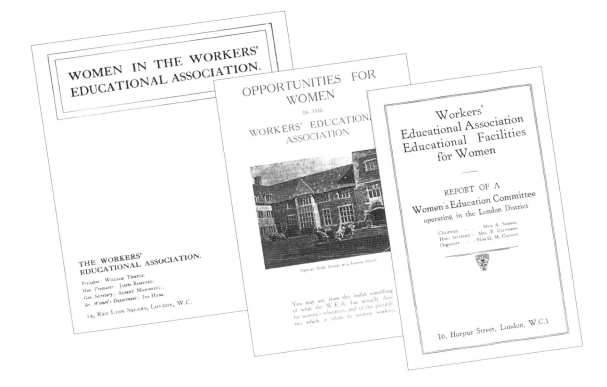

The Students

In the public library ... I saw leaflets about forthcoming classes under the WEA. There were to be two - in history and economics. I joined both; not because I was particularly interested in either, but I would have joined anything. Two lectures and discussions a week were what I now lived for. I borrowed books. Written work was demanded from the students and difficult to get from most of them. To me, in the great press and surge of my longing for self-expression, it seemed a benefaction. To be allowed to write essays! Well, I did write them and I am glad they haven't survived for me to read today. They must have been very bad, I feel now, full of purple passages and attempts at fine writing. Still, I was proud of them at the time.

Marjory Todd, *Snakes and Ladders: an Autobiography* **(1960)**

I didn't eat, I didn't go out – my furthest journey was my washing line. I didn't see anyone. I felt suffocated. I desperately needed to get out of this depression, but there didn't seem a way. I saw my doctor. He gave me iron tablets, vitamins, anti-depressants and a counsellor.

As I started to get my life back into perspective, a letter came, via my child's nursery, from the WEA. It advertised a morning group with a free creche.

I now had two things in my week – the parent Volunteer Training course and my placement in school. This way my lifeline. My brain was occupied again. I felt I was myself.

Michelle Bennett, Rugeley, 1998

Women join WEA classes for quite different reasons: a chance to write, a chance to think, a chance to meet other adults, or a chance to get out of the house and have a break from the kids. At different periods, in different places, one WEA class might appear to be quite unlike another – students have been men, women, all ages and from a wide range of backgrounds. Contrary to the impression which earlier accounts have given, women were the majority of WEA students from as early as the 1920s. We know quite a lot about the very first *tutorial* class students, the people who attended the three year courses which were envisaged as an extension of the university system and viewed as the flagship of the WEA. The tutorial students made a commitment to study for three years, to read in preparation for their classes and submit regular essays. This kind of sustained study was hard, and although both men and women who were managing the physical demands of manual work attended tutorial classes, the women tended to be younger. It was difficult to cope with domestic responsibilities and childcare in addition to the tutorial class. The majority of the women, though, were school teachers, who at that period had no college training, office workers and shop workers.

The classes on offer, however, included more than the tutorial programmes. There were lecture programmes, informal groups involved in drama or singing and short courses which were seen as a gentle introduction which might lead to longer study. One-off lectures and courses were provided for trade unions, church groups, Co-operative Guilds, Labour Party groups, youth organisations and for the general public. For most WEA students the class means a mixed class, but from 1910 onwards there was a large programme of women-only provision, either offered to the general public or organised for women's organisations. WEA women students were, from the earliest years, a varied bunch, although up to the Second World War they would have been more likely to be under forty years, unless they were attending a class for an organisation such as the Women's Co-op Guild.

After the Second World War there was an increase in housewives attending WEA classes. 'The lady with the duster', below, was one of a number of housewives who wrote letters and articles for *The Highway*, the WEA journal, in the post-war period, explaining how they valued their WEA classes. The background to these pleas to be taken seriously was the debate being waged, in the WEA, in which many influential men argued that the WEA was straying from its purpose, as so many of its students were now housewives – not workers. By the '60s there were increasing numbers of women trade unionists taking

WEA classes, since the '70s community development and since the '80s 'Second Chance', family and schools courses have brought working class women into the WEA in larger numbers. Meanwhile the classes organised by WEA branches attracted students who were gradually getting older and perhaps more middle class.

We know some general things about women students from the records, but accounts of individuals' lives, from the earliest years, are harder to find. Those that exist are more likely to be written by women who went on to become active as volunteers in the branches, or to write. Students are the hardest of all the categories of women involved in the WEA to represent here – we have too few accounts for the early years and too little space for the wide range of students in today's classes. These accounts are a selection of accounts of and by women students, over 100 years.

WEA 'working women' attending a Cambridge University summer school, *The Highway*, 1909.

Emmie Lawther c1890s-unknown

This account is part of a typescript, found amongst the records of the North Staffordshire WEA district, apparently written by Emmie's husband, as a record of her political life.

Emmie Lawther began work in the pottery industry at 13 years of age. Always studious and, as a teenager, she attended classes run by the Workers' Educational Association. This may explain her becoming an active trade unionist and a branch secretary at eighteen years of age. This was in the days before the First World War, when being a trade unionist often meant the 'sack'.

She was surprised when she discovered that New Year's Day was a holiday in the Northumberland and Durham coalfield. It was not a holiday in the Potteries and she had vivid memories of being sacked on a New Year's Day. One of her treasured possessions was her fully paid up trade union card for 1912. She helped to collect piece-work prices from some sixty firms in the china section of the industry in seeking to establish the trade union rates throughout the industry.

It was during this period, prior to the First World War, that she became a member of the Social Democratic Federation. This was one of the former organisations of the Labour movement which was to become the British Socialist Party in 1916. In 1920, Emmie won the scholarship provided by her trade union to Ruskin College, Oxford. There were nine other members, all male, who sat the examination. There were some thirty women students at Ruskin but I think she was the only one with a direct trade union scholarship.

Katie Arnold 1889-1971

Janet Arnold, Katie's daughter, and Barbara Sparkes, chairperson of Havant branch, wrote this account for the WEA Women's History Project in 2002.

Katie Elliot was born in 1889, the eldest surviving child of a family of six. Her father was a master carpenter and undertaker. Her mother kept a shop – one half sold china and the other toys – thus establishing the family practice that women worked.

An avid reader from an early age, she would conceal a book in her Victorian underwear and disappear to the outdoor 'facilities' to read in peace. This was to the chagrin of the sister next in line who believed – doubtless correctly – that she was avoiding her share of domestic duties.

In November 1906 Katie started her autograph book. Presumably it had been a birthday present. Included in the jottings from her friends is a reference to the rights of women, the problems of war. Unfortunately many items are undated and or signed by initials only. It was surprising to see an item written in French, a language she did not speak. Sometime around 1908 she was apprenticed to a dressmaker and milliner in Worthing, a position requiring skills and aptitudes she did not possess. She does seem to have made an impression on her fellows in spite of being less than competent. Family history indicates that she was very unhappy and she was soon back in Westbury in Wiltshire.

At this time college training in teaching was not required and she 'learnt on the job' as a pupil teacher. She clearly loved it and seems to have taught in local schools. She was married in 1916 to Albert Arnold who had made an entry in her autograph book in 1909, presumably just before he went to Canada for four years. Immediately after the wedding they left for Chislehurst as her new husband was working as a fitter at Woolwich Arsenal – a vital concern for ammunition for the First World War. She taught a class of forty boys, apparently without strain. She just survived the 'flu epidemic of 1919 and around 1920 they returned to Westbury, in spite of the reluctance of Albert, who wanted to go back to Canada. Albert began working for her father and ultimately took over the business.

Initially 'unemployed', Katie was bored and started doing supply teaching. She was asked when her own daughter was about two if she would take on the teaching of two to three children aged about 4 to 5. This was the beginning of her own school, when she would have up to a dozen children at any one time. Her boast was that no child who left her following their seventh birthday was not able to read – the key she believed to their further education. She would have failed to understand the arguments about the right methods of teaching reading; one adopted the right methods to suit the individual child.

At some point in the 1930s she became interested in the WEA. Westbury was not blessed with many intellectual outlets and the WEA was one area where one was able to hear speakers on a wide range of topics. Nothing deterred her from attending a course of lectures or a one-day school, providing refreshments for the lecturers if required. These activities continued in wartime, meetings sometimes taking place in her not over large living room. Westbury was surrounded by 'camps' and troops of various persuasions came to call, regular soldiers, conscientious objectors, German prisoners of war. There was only one requirement, you had to be interested in what was going on in the world and be prepared to defend your point of view. They were all grist to the mill in her search for knowledge. One was never quite sure how she attracted such a diverse group of people but somehow things just happened.

One of her early 'converts' was Barbara Sparkes (nee Godden) who attended her first one-day school in 1942. She has had an association with the WEA ever since and is now chairman of the Havant branch.

Domesticity came some way down on Katie's list of priorities; she was never a slave to the house. She always acted as if knowledge was more important than dusting and who would disagree? She had two main interests, other than her family, - teaching and the WEA. Nothing pleased her more than discussing education with young teachers and the progress of her ex-pupils. Almost to the end of her life she retained her interest in the WEA and in the ability of the lecturers to shine light on world events.

Edith Hall

Edith Hall wrote this in 1977, for a WEA class in Luton. It is an extract from an account of her life as a child in London until 1939, published as a booklet, Canary Girls and Stockpots, by Luton WEA branch.

Trying to catch up on one's education after a long day at work was very difficult and I well understood my father's problems as he had left school at the age of twelve to start work. Every evening he would pore over Harmsworth's *Encyclopaedia* and a *Self-Educator* and together we went to a class organised by the Workers' Educational Association. I had some difficulty in that when I was a skivvy in a one servant household, there would be the washing up to do when I returned from my night class on my evening off which meant changing back into my maid's clothes and washing up the dirty dishes left from the supper I had prepared before leaving for the class.

But now, with what joy, tired out physically but mentally alert, did my dear dad and I discuss our class together over supper which mother had prepared for us, and she would additionally help us by washing up afterwards.

On one occasion when dad and I, together with other workers who had been compelled to leave school early, were attending a WEA class, we discussed what

books would be interesting and easy to read and would be specially suitable for those who had not read a book since leaving school. Until then I had only read popular periodicals such as *Passing Show, Answers, Tit-Bits, Peg's Paper* and cheap novelettes – and then I was introduced to works by Thomas Hardy.

It has to be said that the weekly *Punch* and other publications of that kind showed cartoons depicting the servant class as stupid and 'thick' and therefore fit subjects for their jokes. The skivvy particularly was revealed as a brainless menial. Many of the working-class were considered thus and Thomas Hardy wrote in *Tess of the D'Urbervilles* that 'Labouring farm folk were personified in the newspaper press by the pitiable dummy known as Hodge ...' and it was in this book that Hardy told the story of Tess, a poor working girl with an interesting character, thoughts and personality. This was the first serious novel I had read up to this time in which the heroine had not been of 'gentle birth' and wealthy and the labouring classes brainless automatons.

This book made me feel human and even when my employers talked at me as though I wasn't there, I felt that I could take it; I knew that I could be a person in my own right.

Hilda Homer

Hilda wrote this account in 1989. It was originally published in North West district's pamphlet, WEA Voices: a Collection of Students' Writings.

'In nature there are neither rewards nor punishments, there are only consequences', so states R G Ingerson. Looking back on 75 years of a happy and successful life, I can heartily endorse these words. Born in the Rhineland, Germany, I met my Yorkshireman in 1931, when I used my school English to interpret for him. I still was attending college at Bonn, and he arranged to meet me after classes during his fortnight's vacation. In August 1933 we married at the register office in my home town Königswinter; we travelled to Cologne the same day to pick up my British passport

at the British consulate there and were back in Leeds, Yorkshire, the following day.

'You can finish your studies at Leeds University,' my husband told me. I attended classes alright, not at Leeds University, but at the Mothers' Welcome Clinic at Bramley, Leeds, where I was instructed in how to handle a baby in anticipation of the arrival of our first son. I managed to engage a babysitter for one night each week, and that enabled me to join the Polyglot Society in Leeds and put me in touch with students of modern languages. Three years later, when our second son arrived, interested people from the Polyglot Society visited me for language lessons in German.

My husband's promotion took us to Accrington in Lancashire in 1938. Having moved to a new place, I had to find some folks of kindred spirit. The WEA advertised classes in the local newspaper so I went along to join a philosophy class. I found that the assembled people were all known to each other and were discussing events and outings among themselves. Shyness is not one of my attributes, so I inquired if they would consider a stranger like myself worthy to join their circle. They couldn't have been more welcoming.

Our tutor, Caradoc Jones, a man of learning, patience and discipline, furthered my thirst for knowledge and influenced my course of studies for years to come. A three year tutorial class was followed by a second three year tutorial class. Essays were willingly written and submitted and returned to me with useful pointers to additional sources and encouragement to read and write more. The discussions in class taught me to marshal my thoughts, to ask relevant questions and to contribute sensible comments.

Later I joined Ralph Ruddock's classes in psychology and again studied this subject for several years. Classes on modern literature followed. With my boys growing up, I needed to know more about British literature. Up to then, my knowledge was confined to Shakespeare, the Brontës, Burns and to the study of *Little Lord Fauntleroy*, a book I read for the German equivalent of the 'O' level examinations. My 'A' level subject in English was Longfellow's *Evangeline*. The tutor, Mr. Lewis, introduced us to T S Eliot and Dr Keith Sagar gave us an insight into the works of D H Lawrence. My mind seemed to blossom with all this new knowledge.

And then there were the summer schools! They really were a godsend for a busy working housewife. For one week, one could be a person in one's own right with no other responsibilities calling for attention, except the further study of a subject close to one's heart. No introductions were needed to get into talk and discussions with other students. A subject gained dimensions not previously considered. Every Bangor summer school was a meeting of

friends and congenial people. My husband was persuaded by my enthusiasm to come along after a while. He greatly enjoyed the music seminars and the social intercourse.

The great event in WEA circles was the yearly reception held by Manchester University. Being greeted by the vice chancellor and invited to attend a seminar, addressed by a well known lecturer, a master of his subject, made us feel like honoured guests.

I consider the training and knowledge I gained as a WEA student a major influence on my life. I soon became a member of the local branch committee, and was elected to represent the Accrington branch at the WEA District Committee, on which I served for many years. I attended as a delegate various conferences and looked after the interests of the WEA for eighteen years on the Divisional Education Committee of the Lancashire County Council. My training to gather my thoughts and to get up, speak up and shut up, promoted me to responsible positions in the local Labour Party and my trade union. I consider one of my proudest achievements was when I was elected to be the chairman of the local branch of the General and Municipal Workers' Union.

The consequences of my WEA studies opened many doors for me. I prepared my own material for a three year course in German for the Accrington College of Further Education, where I taught adults at evening classes for over twenty years. From 1945 to 1950 I taught displaced persons English. This was a most interesting experience, enabling Poles, Ukrainians, Germans and Austrians to acquire enough English to take employment in factories and mills. I still attend the local WEA classes, enjoy new knowledge and meet pleasant people. I take along new members every year and earn their gratitude for introducing them to interesting subjects.

If the future generation does realise that knowledge is more than just obtaining a certificate, they too will support the WEA and the consequences of doing so will be far more helpful to them than they could ever imagine. It certainly worked out that way for me.

'The Lady with a Duster'

...

The anonymous author of this article published it under the title 'A Mind Refreshed', in The Highway, July 1947.

I am a worker, and in that sphere which is so often overlooked – the home. I am also an educated worker, and because of my two sons, to say nothing of my innate love of learning, I wish to remain so, or at least to do my utmost in that direction. Many will appreciate the fact that, for a wife and a mother, there is very little finance to spare for extras which, of course, education, or indeed relaxation of any kind, must be deemed at this stage in one's life. I would find no joy in depriving my children of opportunities by selfish spending, therefore I naturally turn to WEA for my outlet.

This all sounds very serious, but I am coming to the lighter side. For my class I have chosen economics. I have a friend in an important post in a banking firm – she goes to a cookery class in her free time. The mere thought of a make-do-and-mend or cookery class makes me turn pale. Thus, I presume, does instinct balance our lives!

My class is on a Monday, of all days! How I ever get there, and the building is down a long, horrible road where it is *always* cold or wet or foggy or windy, still remains one of this world's miracles.

In preparation I spend every evening (towards midnight!) in the perusal of world affairs with added concentration, in order to digest the matter well, over the weekend. All is, however, continually thrust to the back of my mind by the fact that I must remember that there will be oranges on Monday, and if I fail to be there in time I shall miss the allocation, the same direct uncertainty hangs over the baby's eggs. What are my husband and schoolboy son to take for their lunch as the joint has petered out? I must not forget to open the back gate, or the dustman, already a fortnight overdue, will not be able to get in – and so on *ad infinitum*.

Every dawning Monday is, in all well conducted households, washday, even if one does employ the uses of a laundry later on in the week. If one is an ultra-efficient housewife, the ironing too is done before nightfall, but as I have the excuse of an over-energetic toddler, that possibility is always waived in my establishment. I begin the day by clearing up my husband's week-end untidiness, mainly caused by doing odd jobs to help me. Naturally as fast as I clear up my small son sees to it that Satan shall, at least, find no work for *my* hands. I then turn to the delinquencies of my big son, making mental notes all the time that I *will* train him to be more tidy, and that I must change his school as I feel it lacks discipline.

Thus the day wears on and I wear out, until my schoolboy returns full of school and loving home. Tea over and the baby 'mothered' and bathed, looking as though he could never have committed all those crimes, I pop him into bed, trying hard to recall the whiles something of current affairs and of the principles of political economy. Now to try to disguise the horrid truth that I am a harassed housewife, whilst my elder son dances up and down the garden path to see whether my husband is going to arrive in time for me to catch the bus. He has never failed me yet, and with last minute orders as to what is for supper, what time my son must retire, how carefully he must do his homework, and that there must be not reading in bed after a certain time – I am off!

In the bus I try to relax and to collect my thoughts. Then I am there, and in my element for two hours, though the world would say, I suppose, that I had left my proper element behind me. The return bus I generally catch with my face burning with the fire of interest. (The last class before we broke up for Christmas was so all-absorbing that we forgot to wish one another a 'Happy Christmas'.)

Once within my own front door again, I immediately carry on where I left off, at the same time arguing the evening's topics with my husband. First I dash upstairs to see two sleeping boys, the elder of whom sometimes opens eyes and lips just wide enough to ask, 'How did Ekkers (schoolboy slang) go, Mummie?'

It is a lovely feeling to have got away from household ties for a time, and to know that the 'family' is interested too, even if my husband does sometimes sarcastically suggest that I should take some sock mending along with me! It is also good to know that, as the boys grow up, they perhaps will not consider their mother such a nonentity after all, even if she does spend much of her time at the kitchen sink.

When I was at school many years ago I enjoyed books by 'The Gentleman with a Duster'; I sign myself very humbly and apologetically, and, I feel sure, much more truthfully, as his female prototype.

Brenda Flynn

Brenda wrote this account for the WEA Women's History Project in 2001

My name is Brenda Flynn (née Clarke). I was born in Eccles, Lancashire in 1932, the daughter of licensed victuallers who ran a public house in a working-class area of Salford. In 1943 (the year my father died), I won a scholarship to one of the local Girls' High Schools. Our household now consisted of my mother, my maternal grandmother (who believed that educating girls was a waste) and myself. My brother, married and 12 years my senior, was serving in the Royal Artillery in the Eighth Army.

In 1948, I left school with a Joint Matriculation Board School Certificate in eight subjects, a love of history and an ambition to be a librarian. I found a job in the Manchester branch of Boots' Booklovers' Library, a subscription library patronised by office workers in the city, but still harboured hopes of finding a public library post. A year later, encouraged by a school friend, I took a clerical job with British Railways, where I met my husband who had just finished his two years' National Service. We married in the autumn of 1951 and continued to live in the Manchester area for the next 11 years.

Our daughter was born in 1953 (followed by sons in 1957 and 1959). My time was largely taken up with looking after the children and running the house but I always found time to listen to the radio and to read the daily newspaper and books (often while undertaking others tasks - washing up, feeding the baby). Even during the six years we lived in a village on the edge of the Peak District, where library provision consisted of two bookcases, available only on Monday evenings in a room over the Co-op which smelled heavily of cheese and bacon, I managed to keep up my reading habits.

Although money was tight, I was fortunate in having a small washing machine and (eventually) a spin drier, although hot water was obtained either from a small over-the-sink heater or the gas wash boiler. Up to 1961 we had no bathroom and only an outside W.C. In 1963, we moved to the north-east of England, when my husband, a railway clerical officer, obtained a job in Darlington. My mother died the following year, and in 1965, our third son was born, after which I suffered a long period of depression.

Somehow my husband must have discovered that Durham University Extra Mural Department and the local branch of the WEA jointly offered evening courses and he suggested that I might like to enrol on one. I duly turned up at the school where the courses were then held and joined a local history course. It wasn't a wonderful success as I found that most of my fellow students were old hands and I felt that I knew absolutely nothing about the town's history. Anyway, I stuck it out and went on to join other courses, mostly on the history of the north-east which I found fascinating, but also on the history of architecture and landscape gardening. And, of course, I fell upon the book boxes which were provided and read and read. I also discovered the delights of the local library which besides having a lending section also rejoiced in a reference section and (eventually) a Local Studies Room. It would also be about this time that I became interested in family history and took the first tentative stumbling steps to discovering my roots. In the early 1960s, the study of family history by 'ordinary' people was in its infancy and there was very little available in the way of 'how to do it' books and finding aids. I remember how I set out on my first family history jaunt to Lincolnshire, in great fear and trepidation (leaving my husband to cope with four children for three days): the joy of sitting in a Methodist church and handling the actual register in which my great-grandparents' marriage had been recorded; the thrill of visiting the village in which they had lived and where my grandfather had been born; the panic when I presented myself at the County Record Office with no notion of what to ask for or of what I might be permitted to look at; the suspicion with which a lone woman was met when she tried to book a room in a hotel.

During this time, although basically still a very shy woman, I was gaining in self-confidence and learning that my opinions were equally as valid as those of my fellow students (and, somewhat to my surprise, even those of tutors). I also recognised that, although I might be loath to fight my own corner, I certainly had to be prepared to fight those of my children.

In the early 1970s, women's studies became a popular subject and I enrolled on a 'New Opportunities for Women' course, where I found myself exposed to feminist thinking and rubbing shoulders with fellow students, often younger and better educated than me. Even more unnerving, I was required to write essays, for the first time since leaving school over 20 years before. It was encouraging to discover that I could still do it.

Around this time, I began to consider the possibility of returning to the world of paid employment....It seemed that I should be thinking about contributing to the family budget. But what could I do? What skills had I to offer? I had not undertaken paid work for more than twenty years. I brushed up my typing skills at the local college of technology but our youngest son had developed asthma and was often absent from school with chest problems. With no family members to fall back on for child-minding, I felt that, realistically, I could only look for work which could be fitted around my family responsibilities. I decided to opt for evening work and took a job as an usherette in the local theatre which, under an enthusiastic young director, was just beginning to establish a reputation for excellence. Over the next four years, I welcomed audiences, sold programmes, sweets and programmes, persuaded reluctant patrons that they were sitting in the wrong seats, mopped up the consequences of children's Christmas over-indulgences and even tried my hand at being a theatre dresser....

At the end of the 1970s, with two sons at university and the youngest (his asthma more or less under control) at secondary school, I began to look around for part-time clerical work and found a job as a wages clerk. By this time, my husband had become involved with the WEA, becoming a committee member (subsequently chairman) of the local branch and a part-time tutor. I found myself becoming more and more involved in the social activities of the branch, helping to provide coffee for course students, scones for the Saturday coffee mornings and buffet lunches for Saturday day schools and, need it be said, washing up. In the early 1980s, I, too, became a branch committee member and a delegate to District Council.

In 1984... I returned to the theatre to work in the box office for three years, before becoming the general manager's clerical assistant, the post from which I retired at the end of 1997. During this time, I became a shop steward for UNISON, a member of the union's branch committee and the education secretary. I am currently the secretary of the local UNISON Retired Members' Group.

A Durham University course in palaeography led a small group of four students to continue to practice their newly-acquired skills (under the guidance of the tutor who had run that first local history course back in 1965) to undertake the transcription of early seventeenth century Darlington wills. After several years of hard work and research, we were much surprised and gratified to have our efforts accepted for publication by the Surtees Society in 1994. We were authors!

Somewhere along the way, I had become computer-literate (largely self-taught) and am now happy to pass on what expertise I possess to friends and colleagues. Once I had retired, I was able to spend more time on WEA matters, looking at how computer technology might be applied to branch administration. In 2000, I became the branch treasurer and this year attended national conference for the first time.

Now, with my 69th birthday only a matter of weeks away, I can look back on a life which has been enriched by my involvement with the WEA, whose courses and comradeship helped me to find myself, gave me a liberal education and the confidence to hold my own with my university-educated children and has made me a mine of useless information for my five grandchildren.

Thank you, WEA!

Jill Molnar

Jill wrote this account for the WEA Women's History Project in 2001

I am from Scunthorpe in Yorkshire South district, born in 1939. I first attended a WEA class in 1986. I went past the WEA every day on my way to and from work (loading lorries in a factory), eleven years on 6 to 2. One day I saw the WEA was offering afternoon courses. I went to 'Return to Learn' because it was on. I would have gone to pathology or space travel, if it had been on. I was desperate to find 'something more to life'. The tutor organiser said I was in the wrong class and directed me to the 'Writers' Workshop'. By 1992 I had won several major prizes in writing competitions, including three for radio drama. I got a job as a doctor's secretary/receptionist. He was a bully; he overworked and underpaid me. He said he could not pay me more because 'I knew nothing'. One day he rang his bell for me to pick up his pen. I told him where to put it and left, went to college, then to university and got a BA Hons. 2.1 degree in 1997. I am now a tutor at the WEA attempting to put something back, to encourage people who have also little idea of their own worth. The WEA changed my life.

Kathryn Smith

Kathryn wrote this account for the WEA Women's History Project in 2003.

At eighteen years old I became ill with M.E. and found myself condemned to years of bed and daytime TV! I felt as if my future had been snatched away and to compound this, many of the symptoms I was experiencing convinced me that my brain would no longer work as it once had.

As a way back into life I began attending creative evening classes but it was with some trepidation that I decided to attend a WEA poetry class. I have always loved poetry but was no longer confident of my ability to comprehend it or make any sort of contribution to a class. This fear intensified when I found on arriving that I was by far the youngest person on the course and I tried to hide quietly in the darkest corner of the room!

However the friendly open atmosphere of the class and the enthusiasm of the tutor soon lured me out of my corner. To my amazement I found that I could once again form opinions and contribute to discussions. The boost to my confidence and optimism was fantastic and with some persuasion from my tutor I have even joined a writing group.

Whilst I am still far from well and life can be frustrating at times the WEA has given me an opportunity to do something that I love, as well as rediscovering my ability to think and learn and have some hope of a future. At a time when the Labour government are busy slamming the door to higher education on the poor, the fact that I have been able to do all this whilst existing on benefits makes it even more special.

The Volunteers

Why do people volunteer? It's hard to tell, and of course there are as many personal reasons as there are volunteers. I have always been a student in WEA classes, and have been to at least one course a term since my first child was born, so there is a bit of a feeling of putting something back. It is common that when people just help with some little thing, even washing up their coffee cups after the class, they become caught up in the friendly feeling of the WEA and stay around.

For me, after 40 years as a volunteer it has become a habit, sometimes annoying, sometimes frustrating, always time-consuming...but...I could also say it has provided me with a lifetime of friends, some of whom have become the important people in my life...

Keeping the thing ticking over, volunteers like us still make a difference to people. These days it seems to me that there are not very many BIG IDEAS still about where ordinary folk doing not very spectacular things can make a difference – the WEA is one.

Val Portass, Darlington branch, *Reminiscences from a Branch Secretary*

The volunteers in the earliest days of the WEA were the university academics, the church men, trade unionists and Co-operators, who had met together to found the organisation, rapidly joined by the early students. It was the idea of some of the first students that they could increase the classes and spread the word, by going out themselves and setting up their own classes. They talked to other organisations and influential people, produced publicity, booked rooms and set up meetings, just as WEA volunteers have done ever since. In addition they worked as voluntary tutors or study group leaders. As the organisation grew the WEA developed a voluntary structure, copying that of the trade unions; there were regional districts, each managed by a committee structure that represented the network of branches. Each WEA class, traditionally, elected a class secretary who in the old days took the register and represented the class at branch meetings. WEA volunteers have mostly been people who are active in their local branch and these have been overwhelmingly women.

Women as volunteers have carried the weight of local organising and the commitment lasts often for many, many years. Yet women in the WEA, as elsewhere in society, have been less likely to put themselves forward as branch or district officers. The WEA's voluntary movement is dominated, but not controlled, by women. Women's involvement in the WEA tends to be fluid, to lead on from one thing to another: students find they've become volunteers, tutors get involved with a branch, administrators join classes as students and study for degrees, returning as tutors. Some branch volunteers become involved in district affairs and go on to represent the district at a national level. The volunteers are as varied as the students we recruit.

During the 1980s it became increasingly apparent that many WEA students were on programmes of study which had been set up independently of branches and that these students were not represented within the WEA's democratic structures. A new kind of volunteer, a voluntary educational advisor (VEA), was established, who had been a student on at least one class and who helped to recruit new students and groups, but also might be a voluntary support to tutors in the classroom.

For volunteers the enthusiasm for the organisation can be a mixed blessing: people can be difficult, hours of unpaid work can leave one feeling unappreciated, and, in recent years, the power of the paid workers can overshadow the influence of the local volunteer. The women volunteers here are only a sample of the vast numbers of women who have made many thousands of individual contributions, over the last 100 years.

HOW TO INCREASE THE MEMBERSHIP OF A SECTION.

It has already been seen that an important part of the work of a women's section will be of a missionary character. There are numbers of women in every branch who, having tasted for themselves the good things that the W.E.A. provides, are longing to go out and bring in others—particularly those who need it most—to share in the feast. It would be well that every women's section or committee should draw up a scheme of its own for attracting the women of the district. Deputations to all women's organisations, such as adult schools, Co-operative guilds, trade unions, etc., which have not affiliated, should be arranged for; and it is also most valuable and important that special attention should be given to the social side of the work. Afternoon or evening meetings of a ͏mal and friendly nature might be arranged fortnͤhtly or m͏ parts of the district (if it be a large one). a͏ tackle one street at a tim͏ After ͏

Lavena Saltonstall

Linda Croft, a tutor organiser in Yorkshire North district, has been researching the history of Yorkshire North district and contributes this account written in 2003.

In the early spring of 1911 some 'Letters of a Tailoress' were published in the WEA magazine *The Highway*. It is evident that the writer, Lavena Saltonstall, was passionately concerned about the social issues of the day. She speaks with feeling about the quiet heroism of working mothers who struggle daily to make ends meet; of 'humanity lodged in slums and barrack-like streets; children in filth and rags, women swearing and fighting and selling themselves, men drinking and murdering'; of politicians whipping up feelings against the foreigner for their own electoral advantage.

Running through the letters, too, is a commentary on her own situation in life that reflects on how, in working-class communities, girls are socialised into domestic roles:

'As I am a tailoress many people think it is my bounden duty to make trousers and vests, and knit and crochet and sew, and thank God for my station in life. I am supposed to make myself generally *useless* by ignoring things that matter – literature, music, art, history, economics, the lives of people round me and the evils of the day. They think I ought to concern myself over clean doorsteps and side-board covers....In my native place the women, as a general rule, wash every Monday, iron on Tuesdays, court on Wednesdays, bake on Thursdays, clean on Fridays, go to market or go courting again on Saturdays, and to church on Sundays. There are exceptions, of course, hundreds of exceptions, but the exceptions are considered unwomanly and eccentric people...The majority of girls are brought up by well-wishing parents to earn their living, to become thoroughly domesticated, to behave respectably, go to Sunday school and read religious books, all with a view to one day getting married. The "getting married idea" is the most important one in most girls' lives. No account is taken of the fact that just as faces are different, so are temperaments...

Should any girl show a tendency to politics, or to ideas of her own, she is looked upon by the majority of women as a person who neglects doorsteps and home matters, and is therefore not fit to associate with their respectable daughters and sisters.'

Lavena declares that she herself will not be discouraged. 'I only pass through this world once, and I don't intend to pass through, as a bird flies through the air, leaving no track behind.' These letters are intriguing but they raise as many questions as they answer. Who is Lavena? Is she genuinely a working class operative tailoress? Where did she learn to write? She expresses herself with power and passion - where has this come from? What was her role in the WEA, and what other social movements or political parties was she associated with? In short, is her history discoverable – has she indeed left a track behind?

What follows is a brief outline of what has been discovered so far about Lavena – but there remain many gaps that could only be filled by thorough research in newspapers and the archives of the Labour movement.

At the time of the 1901 census, Lavena was 19 years of age (and therefore born circa 1882) and a machinist fustian clothing worker living with her parents in Hebden Bridge, West Yorkshire. In the early 20th century, Hebden Bridge had a near monopoly of the production of fustian (a hard-wearing cloth of the corduroy type) and of the manufacture of fustian garments. Women were employed on a large scale as machinists. In 1911 there were 1,249 tailoresses in the area, and they constituted 69% of all employed women, and 37% of all females over 10 years of age.

By 1906 Lavena, now in her mid-twenties, had become closely involved with women who were active in trades unions and suffrage activities, notably Lillian Cobbe of Hebden Bridge and Laura Willson of Ovenden near Halifax. Lillian had been the first woman to join the Hebden Bridge Branch of the Amalgamated Union of Clothing Operatives. This was in 1900, and although a handful of other women followed her lead, Lavena was not amongst them. It may be that in 1900 Lavena was not yet sympathetic to trade unionism, as she later said that her prison experiences had confirmed her in socialism, she having formerly been a Tory - but 'what is a cup of tea with a lot of primrose dames once a year?' But in 1906, Lavena helped Laura Willson organise militant action in support of the Halifax tram drivers' strike. In the same year, a Halifax branch of the Women's

Social and Political Union (the militant suffragette group around the Pankhursts) was formed with Laura Willson as branch secretary. In March 1907 a group of working women suffragists travelled down from West Yorkshire to join an attempt to gain admission to the House of Commons. Those arrested included Lavena Saltonstall and Lillian Cobbe. Found guilty of 'pushing, shouting, and trying to get into the House of Commons', they were sentenced to 14 days imprisonment. On her release Lavena went immediately to Peckham to help in the by-election and over the next few months, she frequently took an active role in elections. She also served at least one more term in gaol, spending five weeks in Holloway in April/May 1908.

Meanwhile, Lavena was beginning to practice journalism. Her first attempts seem to have been letters to the local press arguing the case for women's suffrage, but by April 1909 she was writing a regular weekly column for the *Halifax Labour News*. The subjects she took were varied, ranging from local politics to the church and Christianity, commodity speculation, the adult school movement, the police system, vivisection, and the Salvation Army. Some articles are humorous, as when she described the day when she and Laura Willson 'clad in garments of antiquated design with print aprons to cover our dresses', went 'on tramp' with the intention of gaining admittance to a workhouse casual ward. After tramping hard for nine hours without food, Lavena fainted, they gave up and telegraphed home for the train fare back to Halifax.

Halifax WEA branch was formed in 1909 and Lavena was soon involved. In the autumn of 1911, she was a student in a tutorial class on economics and was writing a column called 'WEA Corner' for the *Halifax Guardian* newspaper. In one article she writes wittily about social interdependence and votes for women:

> 'Among other lectures we have had was one wherein we learned that with all our vain talk about individual and British independence, all of us – from the gravedigger and gas inspector down to the mere politicians who are talking twaddle about manhood suffrage – all are dependent upon hosts of people for all our blessings and miseries.
>
> It seems we can neither eat nor be merry without the help of thousands of other people. Shirtmakers, bootmakers, butchers, bakers and candlestick workers, dyers, miners, seamen, growers, weavers, dockyard labourers, engine drivers and hosts of other people and peoples each have to contribute their share before any of

us can call ourselves civilised. Even the Prime Minister has to be indebted to his laundress, charwoman, cook, housemaid and mother before he can – with any dignity - voice his humble and elementary opinion of woman's qualification for a vote.'

By 1913, Laura Willson was vice president of Halifax WEA branch, her husband George was joint secretary and Lavena was *Highway* secretary. At this period, she was very involved with the work of the branch, sitting on various committees and representing the branch at a conference on the Trade Union Act.

In March 1914, a letter appeared in the *Cotton Factory Times* in which Ethel Carnie, a factory hand and journalist, attacked the educational policy of the WEA and accused it of 'chloroforming the workers'. Miss Carnie presented the usual left-wing criticism of the WEA, arguing that its non-sectarian and non-party political stance betrayed the need of the working class for a class-conscious education directed at overthrowing the system.

Lavena responded to the charge and the two women entered into a debate in which Lavena vigorously defended the non-aligned policy of the WEA, saying:

> 'I resent Miss Carnie's suggestion that the WEA educational policy can ever make us forget the painful history of Labour, or chloroform my senses to the miseries I see around me, and I am only one of thousands in like position....Greek art will never keep the workers from claiming their world; in fact it will help them realise what a stunted life they have hitherto led. Nothing that is beautiful will harm the workers.'

From a working woman, it was a stirring endorsement of the work of the WEA, yet within a couple of years, it appears that Lavena may have left the movement. Her name last appears in the minute book of Halifax WEA branch in June 1916 and nothing more is known about her thereafter. It may be that some reader will have come across her name in connection with the WEA or women's suffrage or trades unions elsewhere in the country and so will be able to illuminate Lavena's later life. But for the time being, we are left with an unfinished portrait of a young woman who rebelled against the suffocatingly narrow intellectual horizons then offered to working class girls. She became involved in the WEA through her passionate belief that art, literature, history and music could expand the horizons of the poor and downtrodden and open the doors to liberation and a better world.

Mary Toomer 1884-1974

Account by Zoë Munby drawn from Lincoln WEA Branch booklet, Fancy a Man From Pond Street Knowing his ABC, *1986, with additional information provided by Dick Winter of Lincoln WEA branch*

'When the polling stations first admitted women voters in 1918, a policeman turning up for duty at one Lincoln booth ventured to comment on the punctuality of a lady already heading the queue. "I've been waiting for years!" came the firm reply.' Mary Toomer, suffragist and founder member of Lincoln WEA in 1911, was a formidable force for radical change in the city. She had spoken on several occasions from a soap box in Hyde Park in support of votes for women. Mary settled in Lincoln on her marriage to William Toomer, formerly a London grocer who came to work for Lincoln Co-operative Society. The Co-op let its committee room to the group who met to found the Lincoln WEA branch and Mary attended as a member of the Women's Co-operative Guild. She was branch secretary from 1927 to 1938; stories of another brush with the law, when cycling without lights (but with a candle in a jam jar) on her return from a distant class meeting, suggest that her energy and determination let few things stand in her way. She combined activity in the WEA with motherhood. She and her husband attended classes on alternate evenings, or her two daughters occupied themselves in the children's library when both parents were out in the evening, and then, when the library closed, moved on to the WEA common room, where they could sit at the back and listen to lectures. Mary also managed to get away to attend Oxford summer schools. She had met William Temple, WEA president and later Archbishop of Canterbury, and was influenced by his ideas and felt that WEA work complimented her own Christian beliefs. For many years she ran an 'open house' in the WEA rooms every Christmas Eve, with home made bread rolls, mince pies and large pots of tea. She also took her daughters with her when visiting inmates in the workhouse, with the objective of allowing them to respect people, whatever their circumstances.

During the First World War, as a member of the National Council of Women, she helped organise the Common Cause Soldiers' Rooms for the Lincoln barracks and at the hospital, for wounded soldiers. Later, when the effects of the depression began to hit Lincoln and unemployment levels began to grow, she worked to support unemployed people. Alice Cameron, the Oxford resident tutor, is credited with developing the scheme that became Lincoln People's Service Club but, undoubtedly, its successful operation relied on the energy of women like Mary who contributed hours of unpaid labour. The clubs offered activities for men and women, from boot and shoe repairing groups for men to sewing classes for women. The local authority provided a tutor for the sewing class and Mary acted as volunteer helper, teaching the women how to cut down adult clothes to fit children and later making bibs, overalls and towels for a new voluntary nursery. Mary is likely to have been influential in Alice Cameron's political development: the pair were involved in direct political action in support of unemployed people and against the family Means Test. When Lincoln City Council decided to stop the allocation of coal to unemployed families, Mary and Alice led a protest march that resulted in the decision being overturned. In 1932 land for a communal garden had been lent to the People's Service Club and vegetables and fruit trees were planted. In 1936 alone Mary presided over the manufacture of 160 lbs. of jam, on gas rings at the WEA common room, with her team of helpers.

A council owned house, Roselands, once a children's home, in the village of Scothern, was equipped by the People's Service Club and run by the WEA as a holiday centre for unemployed workers. It also served as a base for WEA residential schools and weekend conferences. Mary would cycle out once a fortnight to help new families settle in. Later the People's Service Club built a holiday centre of its own, a bungalow at Dunholme, which opened in 1935 and was used up to the outbreak of war, when Mary supervised the packing away and demolition of the building.

Mary was a co-opted member of Lincoln Education Committee for thirty years; she paid a visit to every school in the city, each term, by bicycle, until the age of seventy-five. She had been part of a group on the council who campaigned for a nursery school, achieved in 1932. She never lost interest in the school and the logbooks mention her constantly. She organised 'sewing bees' for mothers and when the school went carol singing, they finished up at her home for sandwiches, tea and mince pies. She acted as cover for the head teacher, on an occasion when she had to be absent for an interview. Her Education Committee role helped the WEA to develop courses for Parent Teacher Associations throughout the city. She campaigned long for an adult education centre for the city, which was achieved in 1964.

Colleen Horton

Colleen wrote this account for the WEA Women's History Project in 2002.

In 1945, as a young girl of 16 I became the secretary of Cheslyn Hay Labour Party and from this beginning was groomed as a future councillor. A few years later it was decided that we should have a greater knowledge of local government. This was when my first links with the WEA began.

The local tutor organiser was Will Ingham who lived in Cannock and our lecturer was Jim Homeshaw from Great Wyrley. The meetings were held in Cheslyn Hay Working Men's Club and we studied local government for two terms. I found the classes gave me helpful knowledge especially when, in 1952, I was elected a councillor at the ripe old age of 23.

After 1952, my life revolved around the Labour Party, the Council and our local Methodist Church.

Obviously I didn't have much time for any extra activities as I worked full-time for the National Coal Board until 1966 when I resigned to study for 'O' Levels which I sat in May 1967. I then attended Wolverhampton Teachers' College for day students. I qualified in 1970 and began teaching in Great Wyrley, the village adjoining Cheslyn Hay.

In 1978 I saw an advert for the WEA Cannock Wood branch. I joined the group and have been a student since that time. I have shared many happy and interesting classes since then and have found many friends amongst my fellow students. During the last twelve years I have served on West Mercia District Committee and in November 2000 I was elected as the chairman of West Mercia district.

Rita Bannister 1922-1998

This account was written by Vicky Moss, Newcastle WEA branch, for the WEA Women's History Project in 2002.

In a letter to Richard Copley, West Mercia district secretary, written in 1994, Rita explains that she has served for 11 years as Newcastle and Wolstanton WEA branch secretary as well as having several other spells as secretary over the past 30 years. Now at last she firmly declines to stand again for election but ends with the words '... I shall hope to continue in the movement as I cannot envisage life without the WEA, perhaps unfortunately, the price one pays for dedication! Seriously, the WEA has been the mainspring of my life for over forty years and the source of much pleasure through lasting friendships to say nothing of the wealth of splendid tuition and stimulating learning.'

Rita Holland was born in 1922 and grew up in Hartshill, Stoke-on-Trent, her father being a painter at Minton's well known for his exquisite small-scale painting on china. There was no possibility of Rita or her two

brothers going to university. During the war she was working in the City Treasurer's Department. She would sometimes spend her lunch break in the balcony of the adjoining hall listening to rehearsals of some of the great orchestras which had been evacuated to the provinces. Sir Thomas Beecham she particularly remembered. About this time she joined a WEA literature class in Longton and literature remained her abiding interest for the rest of her life. In 1947 she was among eight members of this class, most of them in their twenties, who attended a never-to-be-forgotten summer school at Balliol College, Oxford.

She must have been thrilled when in 1949 she was seconded to help the newly appointed librarian of the University College of North Staffordshire, then being set up. He began with a desk in an office beside the town hall in Stoke but when he moved into Keele Hall he took Rita with him as his secretary. Her loyalty to him was absolute in spite of what must have been frustration caused by his reluctance to have any letter or document filed. Rita continued as librarian's secretary until her retirement in 1982, becoming acquainted with most of the academic staff, many of whom came to rely on her helpfulness.

As pioneers in a new venture the administrative and support staff at Keele built for themselves a thriving social life in which Rita took full part. She also contributed enthusiastically to the dances, parties and outings organised in those days by the WEA branches and was a keen member of the Newcastle Gramophone Society and later of the National Trust, making further friends through its local supporters' group. She remained with her parents in Hartshill until her marriage in the mid 1970s. Life at home in the 1960s, however, was not easy for Rita and her father since over several years they were caring for her mother who had been made immobile and incontinent by a stroke.

Nevertheless she was by now an active member of the Newcastle WEA branch, taking her turn as secretary and participating in the affairs of the North Staffordshire district. In 1965 she became branch representative on the District Executive Committee and in 1967 and subsequently was branch representative on the District Council. In 1969 together with Margaret Powell and Eve Rowley she represented the district on the WEA National Council. She remained a personal district subscriber after North Staffordshire amalgamated with the West Mercia district. She frequently attended courses at the Wedgwood Memorial College at Barlaston and was on

its governing body. More recently she was a keen supporter of its courses on the cities and monuments to be explored through foreign travel. After her mother died she greatly enjoyed her trips abroad.

Rita's brightness and optimism made her seem indispensable to the Branch Committee and she was always on the alert for new ideas for courses and for day schools. When she stepped down as branch secretary I took over from her for four years, encouraged by the fact that she was to remain on the committee as president and would be on hand as a friend to guide and advise. My successor voiced what I had felt too, that she was doing the job 'for Rita's sake'. Rita continued to attend literature classes with undiminished enthusiasm although she said once that often she did not have much idea of what the tutor and some of the class members were talking about. I guess post-structuralism was not for her. She had a modest estimate of her own intellectual ability together with a tendency to exaggerate that of others. Nevertheless she held to her quest for wisdom and enlightenment through books.

Enthusiasm was Rita's outstanding characteristic, but those who knew her well noticed another; she rarely, if ever, spoke in negative terms of anyone. After her sudden and shockingly unexpected death in February 1998 many friends spoke of individual acts of kindness. A tree was planted in her memory at Barlaston and the Newcastle branch presented a garden bench which overlooks the arboretum.

Kath Ryder

This account was written by Kath, Swindon WEA Women's branch, for the WEA Women's History Project in 2002.

I was born in December 1932 in Leeds, Yorkshire – then a city largely concentrating on engineering and clothing manufacture. My father was unemployed at the time but later worked on the railway as a platelayer and my mother was at home looking after my two older sisters, who were only two and three years old at the time. Home at that time was a back to back terrace house in the poorest part of town. We later moved around to better rented housing as and when my parents could afford it.

My sisters and I were evacuated in 1939, but only stayed a couple of weeks as we were so unhappy. My father died in 1942 and mother struggled on state benefit, trying to keep two of us at High School.

By then I had won a scholarship to High School and after four years gained my School Certificate. I stayed on at school into the sixth form but due to ill-health was unable to continue and left to find work as an office junior, studying shorthand and typing with a neighbour until I was able to go for a better job.

After working in a variety of offices in Leeds I got married and moved to Halifax, where I found office work until my eldest daughter was on the way in 1958. Our house in Halifax was almost on the edge of the moors and we found the winters very hard going. When my husband found a better job opportunity in Swindon I was happy to move south! It helped that my sister had moved to Swindon as a teacher but I did find it a bit difficult at first to fit in. I found that dinner down south was an evening meal, not lunchtime as I was used to – I'm afraid that even now I think of dinnertime as 12 noon – and the different names for types of bread and even cuts of meat were a puzzle.

My first experience of the WEA came at that time, when I noticed an afternoon course which was running with a crèche – pretty unusual in the '60s. The crèche was a lifesaver and I'll always be grateful to the WEA, though I confess I've quite forgotten what the subject of the actual course was.

Some time later I heard a talk on the life of Reuben George, who instigated the Swindon WEA branch in 1909, and I was very impressed by the tale of his enterprise and dedication to the ideal of bringing higher education to the masses at a time when only the privileged few could afford it. No doubt this talk, together with my experience of the crèche, predisposed me towards WEA classes when I started looking for evening classes later.

My next real involvement with WEA came in the late '70s as a result of attending joint WEA/University classes relevant to the committee work I was then engaged in for the Pre-school Playgroups Association. A student newsletter appealed for help on the WEA committee and I felt able to respond as my time to move on from PPA was approaching.

Early in my time with the WEA committee I had the opportunity of attending a special national day conference in London on the topic of women's education and that did it – I was inspired by the possibility of working within the WEA specifically to help women who had missed out on educational opportunities and who were experiencing a time in their lives when confidence was at a low ebb. My own time of shattered confidence had been as a young mother, even though I had a good husband beside me and a reasonable education at my back.

I joined the Swindon Branch Committee, became secretary and encouraged the work with women's groups – eventually forming first a women's sub-committee and later hiving off as a separate branch attracting funding from outside. The male tutor organiser for the area had initiated work with women's groups and the male project worker for the unemployed helped us by moving across money which he had for working with women (whom his project was not attracting).

Needing to fight the prejudice within parts of the Association against what we were doing I attended District Council regularly, got elected to District Committee and have been involved there ever since, with two stints as chair and one as treasurer. I have been a member of the NEC for a number of years and involved in national Women's Education Committees – first when Eileen Aird was national officer and again when WEC was formed.

The Swindon Women's branch has been going for eighteen years now and is privileged to receive funding from the Borough Council in recognition of the work we do.

Jill Arnold

Jill wrote this account for the WEA Women's History Project in 2001.

Most of my memories of the incidents and events of how I became involved with the WEA are still vivid and easily recalled. Yet in trying to conjure up a picture to portray my experiences, and those of other women, from twenty years ago, what was hard to recall was just what it was *about* what happened that explains why I continued to work so hard and devoted so much of my time and energy to the Association for the next twenty years. In my first brief encounter with the WEA in the early '70s, a time of love and revolution, I'd been inspired by students who had been through the WEA and Coleg Harlech to study at university and full of ideas and enthusiasms for learning as a means of liberation and change....

Ten years later I found myself living near the small market town of Melton Mowbray in the East Midlands out of paid work and with two small children. The Thatcher regime was already beginning to oppress women's lives in ways that we couldn't possibly have imagined in the '70s days of struggle for liberation. So, the discovery that there was a WEA branch *and* that it was putting on a short daytime course entitled: 'Women and Health' (women only *and* with crèche provision) was a welcome surprise. It turned out to be more than just a class – it saved my life!

This class was a model for the kind of inclusiveness and openness that is the benchmark of excellence in adult education and life long learning. Along with the other women I found inspiration from the tutors, from the stuff we were learning (knowledge/experiences about our bodies/ourselves, for women, by women) and from each other. Here were women tutors who knew what women's education could/should be about, were good at their work and could make learning such a worthwhile experience. It was a good time (in the worst of times) for joining things and starting a revolution.

Such was our success, our energy and demand for more classes, that Monday mornings became established not just as a 'slot' for women's classes but a starting point for change in all our lives and it was some kind of revolution. The work that followed (both inside and out of the WEA) went against the grain of the political and cultural times. We discovered our psychology, history, literature and the impact of the way the media and institutions portrayed and represented us. We learnt that learning is about being changed not just about 'acquiring' knowledge and that learning gives personal confidence but it most definitely was also political! Issues, ideas, politics and actions sprang from them - crèches as a regular provision, venues to suit women, organising courses for women 'returners'. Also – (and reflecting our preoccupations then as young mothers) we started a Birth Group, campaigning to save the maternity unit at the local hospital, starting democratically run mother toddler groups. The other major effect of the class was to recharge our ideas about our work prospects (or what might pass for a career - often broken with having children, or from peering at the light through glass ceilings). We learnt to have confidence to return, to begin, to take up training or go for further and higher education. Most importantly we learnt to value our social and personal experiences and lives as women: working in and as part of our communities, getting things done, inventing ways and means, changing things, writing things, pestering people and starting things.

Does this all seem to be enough to keep me in the WEA for 20 years? Possibly - but sometime, early on in the life of Monday group, I also volunteered to go to a branch planning meeting to put forward our ideas for future courses. I was shocked to find that the WEA was still (mostly) men in suits (and mostly founder members) who though polite, respectful and friendly and generally very encouraging (if rather patronisingly) about the day time sessions, did not seem to be a WEA that would support all our ideals and aims. I did though catch a glimpse of the possibilities for women as voluntary members in an organisation that 'let things happen' to 'see how they developed'! Inspiration also came from a branch member who told me that he was pleased that the branch was supporting us as the WEA, even a small branch, should be thinking globally! I knew what he meant and it is still something I aspire to and work on. I eventually found there were opportunities to be seized in all layers of the WEA (branch, district, national), in volunteering for roles (chairing committees, editing *Tutors News, or County Newsletters*); in trying to influence aspects of the WEA's organisation (women's education, educational policy, joint work with the universities, creating accredited courses, media appearances) that enabled us to support women in their learning and their lives, locally and occasionally even globally.

There was of course the struggle to keep the WEA alive (or with women to keep their local project going) that meant we were engaged with the rampant individualism and market led policies of the times that particularly disadvantaged women. So in adversity we supported each other and ourselves (through local WEAG (Women's Education Advisory Group) and the work of WEC (Women's Education Committee)) and we had the best times at the best conferences, day schools, workshops, newsletters, doing things, starting things and making connections....

Perhaps I do remember now why I stayed. I was inspired as women spoke out for the first time at national conference about women's issues; pleased when we got funding for classes for women isolated by lack of opportunities in rural communities or inner cities, or for creating a partnership with women from an ethnic minority group. I was supported through friendship in planning integrated women's studies programmes with colleagues, or devising courses for women 'returners'. Then working as a member of WEC, and getting women's education a priority area of work nationally. The list is long and they all now blur into so many achievements for women in the WEA, and the work we did. I claim in my CV that all my work is infused with and informed by what I learnt from the WEA and from struggling to

contribute something in this chauvinist world. The WEA's values, ideals and respect have sustained me and become part of who I am and what I do....

It's probably still hierarchical as well as democratic and preposterously chauvinist whilst working very hard to provide the widest curriculum to the broadest constituency. It may not always see women's education work as mainstream, but I think I've remembered why these contradictions didn't stop me and other women working in the WEA. It tolerates things happening at its edges and it's not afraid of work that's ideologically driven! Twenty years ago we were supported enough to springboard things to happen and spark off other activities. There were disappointments and frustrations but the WEA offered me and other women real friendship and provided structures that enabled us to achieve *our own goals* and make our own differences. I know the WEA will go on finding a home for women who contribute by keeping the faith, wearing the red petticoats and refusing to retreat from trying to get the work done out there we know should be done and that can be done and having learnt go off and start other revolutions.

Happy Birthday sisters in the WEA.

Betty Toland

This account was written by Betty for the WEA Women's History Project in 2003.

I suppose you could call me self-taught; my mother was an avid book reader and taught me to read at the age of four. My life ever after was full of Enid Blyton and then progressed to Jane Eyre. Yes, I took in enough maths to get by and 'Global Warming' was out of my vision. The Soviet Socialist Republic was far away from my small village of Verwood, which was my world.

Leaving school at fifteen I took a job as office junior for an estate agency which was in the next town. My formal education finished and family life, marriage and children took over. Out of necessity I returned to work at the age of twenty-five as a ward maid in the local hospital and I joined the union as insurance against any unforeseen trouble that may come my way. After many years in healthcare, whilst working as a healthcare assistant, I received a leaflet through my letterbox from Unison telling me of a course called 'Return to Learn'. It seemed like a good idea at the time and despite an awful lack of confidence that had developed over the years and weeks of uncertainty about my ability to learn, I went along to the information evening.

And so my journey began and I was about to discover my brain again. With the help of my WEA tutor I started out on a new journey of discovery that made me feel able to question. It felt like being a child again and the words why? how? when? were always on my lips. Fortunately I also learnt that it was all right to question things and nobody looked at me as if I was an idiot. Sometimes, I was even thanked by the members of the group who were not as inquisitive as I was. Later, I changed the word inquisitive to brave. It takes a lot of bravery and courage to admit one's shortcomings and try once again in this strange environment of learning. I progressed through the ten-month course and soon it

was time to receive my praise and accreditation. I was so pleased with my achievements and with the encouragement of my friends and family, I decided to look into the possibility of becoming a voluntary education advisor; I wanted to help others feel like I had and help them achieve their dreams. The advisor course was for two years and taught me things like mentoring skills and different teaching methods. I was happy watching the excitement of the new 'Return to Learn' students as they followed the path I had gone down a few years before, and soon I had supported several tutors and many students, never without the thrill of learning with them and, of course, making the tea! Tea breaks often provide an opportunity for friendships to develop and lighter subjects to be introduced to the conversation.

During this time I also took a pilot course with Unison/WEA and The Open University called 'Issues in Society Today'. This was another different learning experience and took me a little further from the sheltered classroom I was used to. I followed this course with another, a 'Foundation in Social Science', completing the first half and then not having sufficient funds to continue; maybe one day I will complete it.

I have made many friends during my seven years with the 'Return to Learn' course and learnt so much. I am still supporting a group in Bournemouth and still experience the same joy in being there. The pleasure I get from the thank you cards and letters I receive and often the news that someone has fulfilled a lifetime's ambition is beyond description.

'Return to Learn' has changed my social life and, with my new found confidence, I have discovered some hidden talents and now perform with the Bournemouth Shakespeare Players. It seems strange that one leaflet can do all these things. Every one deserves a second chance and that is how I see 'Return to Learn'.

The Tutors

Remembering that my students had been at work all day in the mills and that being mostly married women, they had many other duties as well, I wondered how on earth I was going to hold their interest for such a long time, so late in the evening. I need not have troubled myself. They not only stayed the course but, at the close of each class, accompanied me down the street to the railway station still arguing and discussing, stood on the platform while I, my head out of the carriage window, continued the class, and made their last contributions to the discussion in shouts above the roar of the train as it pulled out of the station. Can you beat it?

Maude Royden, describing a women's Shakespeare class in Oldham, 1908-9.

At first the students were silent, they did not laugh, comment or ask questions. I found this disconcerting; it meant I had to keep on talking. As they became more used to me, they were somewhat more forthcoming though most remained reserved...There were usually more men than women. In one class the only woman was the village school mistress who acted as class secretary. She was well able to hold her own; but most women students were shy and silent. Some brought their knitting, as if to signal that they were spectators, not participants.

The members of (one) small village class asked me to teach them how to discuss, which I did. They became very good at it, the women as much involved as the men. This was unusual. In most village classes it was the men who talked. I remember one woman whose thoughtful and penetrating remarks were made in a vague, detached manner, as if indicating that they need not be taken seriously. In one class, the women sat apart, even the married couples separated; in this class the women hardly ever spoke.

Rachael Young, account of teaching WEA classes for Cambridge University Extra Mural Board, from 1945, in Norfolk.

The great challenge for all teachers is to involve their students and create such an interesting class that they want to return each week. For tutors within workers' education there has often been a wide gap – of education and class - between the experience of the teacher and the taught and creating that magic has been hard. The first women who taught WEA classes were employed by the universities, to teach the tutorial classes which were devised as the 'new idea' of WEA education, a way of bringing higher-level study, with a commitment to essay writing and three years of study, to working people. Some of the people who taught tutorial classes were academics with an existing post at a university; most were new, younger graduates, often inspired by radical or Christian ideals. They got work if a local committee requested a particular tutor; women found it hard to break into a world where serious university-level study was assumed to be a male preserve. If the women tutorial tutors taught predominantly women-only classes, this was as much a product of prejudice as positive discrimination.

From an early period the local WEA committees which sprung up also began to organise their own, local, class programmes: initially these did not earn grants and relied on voluntary tutors. The middle class people with the confidence and time to offer their services included vicars, school teachers and also women, some of whom were graduates with few employment prospects. Other voluntary tutors were the tutorial class students themselves, including women, who took study groups and classes, passing on the lectures they heard from one week to the next. Women tutors remained in the minority, except for women-only classes.

During the Second World War women replaced men as tutors, as they did in every other profession, and, as in other jobs, were squeezed out again when the troops returned. By the late '60s the impact of full employment and increased educational opportunities meant that part-time teaching was less and less attractive to men, and there existed a growing band of women, often returning to work after having children, who were looking for part-time work. The WEA tutor was now more likely to be an early-retired man or woman, or a young woman with children. By the '70s tutors posts began to be filled by young graduates, especially in the expanding work with trade unions; some of these were women. There are no reliable figures but by the 1980s increasing numbers of WEA tutors, if not the majority, were women.

Apart from those women who went on to university posts we know very little about the early women tutors, even less about the working class voluntary tutors. Those who left behind memoirs tended to be the women whose lives expanded to include political or academic careers. Women tutors worked with the difficulty of reaching their classes, let alone teaching: travelling, often at night, to out of the way places, on public transport. They have had to navigate the uncertainties of part-time work and teaching with few resources and little support. Coming to the work sometimes by accident, because it fitted around childcare or because they had rejected other teaching roles, their methods have often been innovative: developing new materials, drawing on students' own memories, experiences and interests.

The woman tutor is more likely to be an unknown, but locally loved figure, over-shadowed by some illustrious men who have used the WEA as a stepping stone to academic or political fortune. Students often tell us that a class has changed their life: here are just few of the women who've been part of that transformation.

SOME SUGGESTIONS FOR WOMEN'S WORK IN THE FUTURE.

How the sphere of work might be enlarged.—We believe that through Girls' Clubs much might be done to get our women to care about education, while they are still young. The members of these clubs are, as a rule, extra-ordinarily intelligent, and interested in many things, though often easily frightened by a mere title. The secretary of a girls' club said she thought her girls would enjoy a literature class. When the proposed teacher went down to the club to talk the matter over with the girls themselves, they di not at first respond at all to the idea. "Literature ! Whatever's literatu" they asked ; " literature would be too hard for us." But when the that literature might mean learning about Scott 1 Dicker writers like them, that it might mean reading cussing which peo which peo they h

Maude Royden 1876-1956

This account by Zoë Munby draws on Sheila Fletcher's Maude Royden, *1989 and Maude's articles in* The Highway.

Maude was born in 1876, the daughter of an affluent Liverpool ship owner and the youngest of eight children. Born with both hips dislocated, she was lame throughout her life and the tiredness and her sense of her own ugliness that this created contributed to her identity as the under-dog in the family. Maude was allowed to chose her own schools and her parents accepted her desire to study history at Oxford, however unusual this was felt to be. 'I was born a feminist and thought myself as good as anyone.' Returning home, after university, she began working as a volunteer at the Liverpool Women's Settlement, and running a girls' club.

She was, however, uncomfortable with charitable work. Through a friend she met the charismatic Oxford extension lecturer, Hudson Shaw, who became her mentor and with whom she was eventually to set up home in a celibate, if rather extraordinary, threesome with his wife Effie. Shaw persuaded the Oxford Delegacy – the body that organised lectures outside the university ('extension lectures') – to try Maude as a lecturer in 1903 and her work grew to include tutorial classes for the WEA. She was the first woman to be appointed as a lecturer to the Delegacy and her WEA classes, although she taught for only a few years, made a major impact on her students. Her powerful speaking style and passionate engagement with her subject –'I am burning to start Shakespeare classes all over the kingdom' – bewitched the women-only classes that frequently demanded Maude as their teacher. She made the case for education rise above the everyday '...we have so little, *too* little, of human interest in our lives at all. The routine of labour, the drudgery, the mechanical repetition, the physical exhaustion, the crushing, the narrowing anxiety for the future; these are what "life" means to too many toilers. They are given all too little leisure for the human side of things, with its beauty and graciousness, its common *ordinary* joys, its consecration. Well, the women are asking for Shakespeare and poetry – because it is so near to life – and because it is so far away.'

Moving back to Oxford in 1905 Maude attended her first suffrage meeting and from that time until 1914 her energies were focussed on the fight for the vote. She wrote extensively, in the WEA publication, *The Highway*, and edited *The Common Cause* for the National Union of Women's Suffrage Societies, promoting wider women's issues as well as the vote. She was a popular public speaker on suffrage platforms and began to campaign for social purity, speaking on subjects such as child abuse and prostitution, at a time when this was difficult for any woman, and more so for a single one.

At the outbreak of war Maude joined those women who saw support for war as at odds with her feminist values and she became active in the international women's peace movement. In 1918 she adopted a baby girl, Helen, and set up house with her old friend from university, Evelyn Gunter. In 1921 she adopted a four year old boy, Friedrich, an orphan of the Austrian famine. Evelyn acted as 'mother' to the two children and Maude threw her energies into what was to be the over-riding enthusiasm of her last thirty years, the ordination of women. She used her public speaking skills, developed in adult education, to preach and speak for a transformation of women's place in the Church of England.

In 1944 Shaw's wife died and Maude married her eighty-five year old lover, who died himself two months later. Maude lived until 1956.

Ethel Lennard 1887-1969

This account was written by Zoë Munby using family history sources and The Highway.

Ethel Lennard was born in 1887 near Halifax. Her father was a vicar and her mother was herself a vicar's daughter. Ethel grew up in the rectory at Heyford, a village in the Oxfordshire countryside. She was taught at home and later at a convent school, eventually studying for a chemistry degree at Oxford. Her situation there reflects the difficulties experienced even by privileged middle class girls. A testimonial from her tutor stated, 'She was severely handicapped by having had no previous experience whatever of scientific subjects before coming up to Oxford; but an unusual natural ability, combined with great zeal and determination has helped her to overcome what, in so many similar cases, has proved an insurmountable obstacle.' Ethel had wanted to train as a doctor, but as the family was opposed, she set about gaining the necessary experience for a career as a factory inspector. From when she graduated, in 1910, she appears to have taken sanitary inspectors' examinations and made good some of her ignorance of working class lives in offering volunteer lectures for the WEA. Ethel's older brother, Reg, was at this time an Oxford lecturer, and it is probable that he was the source of her introduction to the WEA.

In January 1913 *The Highway* reports her teaching an economics class at High Wycombe and a history class at Ascott-under-Wychwood, a village with a rich tradition of radicalism, women's education and, at this period, with a pioneering mother and baby clinic. Ethel began working as a factory inspector in 1914, quite soon being moved to the north. In 1917 she married a Leeds surgeon and gave up her post. She had four children and she never took up a career again. In later years she ran a small farm and involved herself in parish and rural district council work for the Labour Party; she does not appear to have re-made connections with the WEA although her oldest son, and two of her granddaughters, followed her into adult education and taught WEA classes.

Alice Cameron 1891-1964

This account by Zoë Munby is based on Lincoln WEA Branch booklet, Fancy a Man From Pond Street Knowing his ABC, *1986; The* Woman's Who's Who, *1936; the Alice Cameron collection at The Women's Library and information from Somerville College, Oxford.*

Alice grew up in London and studied at Oxford before the First World War, where she was influenced by the ideas of A.D. Lindsay, whose Christianity and philosophy had impressed a generation of university adult tutors. She worked as a war probationer from 1914-16. She was organiser of the Federation of Women Workers from 1916-18 and lectured at Bangor University from 1920-21. She became the Oxford resident tutor at Lincoln, teaching WEA classes from 1921, carrying on the work of her predecessor, Helen Stocks. Alice was determined to maintain an elevated intellectual standard and offered philosophy courses; when asked to teach literature, she agreed, on condition the set book was Plato's *Republic*. However, she was also able to respond to students' individual needs. Kate Mumby, who had left school at ten years to look after her brothers and sisters, was taught to read and write by Alice, and later went on to gain a scholarship to Oxford, graduating at forty years and becoming a tutor herself. In the early '30s Alice took a group of six WEA men on a week's trip to Paris.

The levels of unemployment at Lincoln by the late '20s were high and the WEA branch wanted to do something about a situation where skilled men were left with time on their hands. Inspired by Lindsay's ideas for social service, Alice supported the branch in organising an exhibition of handicrafts made by unemployed people, and together they began to develop the idea of a workshop for unemployed people. The scheme, which in 1928 became the People's Service Club, was a collective effort, managed by a committee of the WEA, but one that Alice worked to establish. She had lobbied for support from the Ministry of Labour, local officials, the trade unions, the WEA and a local trust. They established a programme that included boot repairing for unemployed people, a woodwork class producing furniture for the workhouse and toys at Christmas for disabled children. There was a women's dress-making class. The club eventually supplied free resources for organisations all over the country - unemployed clubs, children's homes, first aid boxes for St John's Ambulance brigade, collecting boxes for the hospital, commodes, bed rests and invalid chairs for sick people. The club was a model for schemes developed throughout the country, and lasted ten years.

The People's Service Club was a partnership, more directly, between Mary Toomer, a working class WEA activist, (see Volunteers) and Alice. Mary's direct political experience was to influence her more reserved colleague

From 1929-1930 Alice studied in America on a Rockefeller Fellowship. Her work with the WEA at Lincoln finished in 1940 and she worked during the war years for Lambeth Borough Council. From 1945 to 1951 she worked in Germany for the Allied Control Commission and the YMCA, developing citizenship and local government education and working with women's groups. Back in England she worked for the Foreign Office School for Germans. She published *In Pursuit of Justice* in 1946.

Janet Cockerill

Janet wrote this account, an extract from a longer autobiography for her family, in the 1990s. As Janet Walters she worked as WEA resident tutor in Northamptonshire from 1943-46 and was resident tutor organiser in Essex from 1952-54. She has also worked for the Council for Education in World Citizenship, for the BBC and was principal of Hillcroft College, a residential adult education college for women, from 1964-1982.

In the summer term of 1943 I was trying to make up my mind what work – from the very limited choice available for someone in my situation – I might take up when I graduated from Oxford in June. I went to a meeting on the subject of the WEA, about which I knew nothing. There I met Frank Jacques, secretary of the Eastern district, an informal but very good speaker and from that meeting, and a long conversation I had with him in a pub afterwards, I emerged fired with enthusiasm and a conviction that I could help to prepare people for all the complications with which the post-war world was going to face them and give them a push in the direction of the fairer society that I wanted to see come about. I had little idea at the time that Frank, in solving my problem, was also solving one of his own. In order to keep the WEA in being when all his male tutors were being called up, he needed to recruit women, who unlike the men could be granted reserved occupation status, to keep a pattern of adult education classes going whilst the war lasted and thus help preserve the future of the WEA, to which he was devoted.

So in the September, after a week's induction course, I found myself a resident WEA tutor in Northamptonshire along with three other equally green graduates. Our immediate contacts in Northants were two splendid men from the boot and shoe industry – one the union officer for the county and the other Arthur Allen, chairman of the county WEA, who became an MP in 1945. It was Arthur who helped me with the problem of digs.

The house in St Peter's Avenue, Kettering, was the home of the two Miss Greens. The elder, known to me as 'Miss Say', had once been parlourmaid to the Dean of St Paul's in London. By now old and frail, she still laid the table for lunch with meticulous care for the sake of their lodgers – a bank clerk, a potato merchant who came and went, a young engineering apprentice and me. She shuddered occasionally at the slapdash habits of Miss Sophie, her energetic and much younger sister, who did the cleaning, the washing (she once inadvertently dyed the bank clerk's pyjamas bright yellow and he was furious) and the cooking and could still sit down to lunch and take a taster with the serving spoon from the communal stew she had prepared. It took me a while to put together the reason why Miss Sophie had welcomed me – an adult education tutor – so kindly, for she did not speak of her past experiences, except once to mention proudly but without explaining the circumstances that she had been for a short time a student in America at Bryn Mawr. Gradually from other people I learned that very early on, as a young factory worker, she had been inducted into the WEA and had become its first woman working-class organiser. She had been very active and successful, with fertile ideas for innovative work amongst the people she knew so well.

She was very kind to me, understood that I was liable to come home at all hours and would much appreciate the remains of a fire with food and a hot drink left out for me, never minded that I did not feel able to get up early in the morning or that I worked in the sitting room all day until it was time to leave for one of my evening classes.

On my arrival in Northants I had found my winter programme of teaching laid out for me. I, whose subject had been history and who had got as far as Disraeli and Gladstone but no further, was to take classes on 'Current International Affairs' and 'The Problems of the Post-War World'. Each weekday night I was to go to five different WEA branches in turn; and each seemed to be following a somewhat different syllabus. Later on I was able to branch out to other subjects of study about which I did know something, for student appetite was omnivorous, but to begin with I had my work cut out to keep one step ahead, particularly as the Kettering public library had limited resources and I was only allowed to borrow two books at a time. So many years afterwards, I can now confess that I took to borrowing others without permission but I did meticulously always take them one day and put them back on the shelves the next. I wonder now if the librarian knew what I was up to and resolutely ignored it. From the material available I read all day long, usually continuing by the dim black-out on the bus journey to my class. I never had time to write a script, nothing but the most rudimentary headlines to guide me through an evening's work. This was excellent training for me and seemed to be acceptable to the students.

For the first winter I had no car and a good deal of my time was taken up with horrendous journeys. Workmen had priority tickets on the buses so that in order to be sure of getting on a bus to a place where I was to hold a seven o'clock class it was necessary to queue before four o'clock in the afternoon when the factories closed. In fact, the journey would take only half an hour to an hour. So I had plenty of time to waste before my meeting started. Occasionally I walked round and round a village or lurked in the churchyard, sometimes the caretaker would let me into the infant classroom where we were to meet but most often the group members would take it in turn, bless their hearts, to entertain me to tea. Getting home after the meeting was equally varied since by that time the buses had long since stopped for the night. I waited an hour in a country lane for a colleague driving from her own group to pick me up. I had lifts on motorbikes. I borrowed bicycles to get to the nearest station – one night I ran to get to the down platform for a train, careered up a flight of steps and fell headlong down the other side ... but I caught the train.

The following year I had had enough of these journeys and I bought an Austin 7 car for £80. My local garage became accustomed to frantic calls for help. I suppose my main trouble was that I only had one driving lesson before embarking on my winter journeys and I lacked a certain amount of skill! And it is difficult now to convey how hazardous driving was at that time, how dark the blackout made everything, especially on strange roads, and how little illumination blacked-out headlights gave, particularly when the battery was weak. I had innumerable adventures.

Frank had issued us all with the dictum that the tutor was always at a class even if no students turned up and I always did get to mine somehow – and there were always students there waiting. It was the students who made it all worthwhile and I remember some of them to this day. They were splendid in their

devotion and their variety. There were housewives and factory workers and men from the gravel pits, who came straight from work in all their muck and sometimes dozed off from utter weariness no matter how hard I tried to make the meeting lively and interesting. Actually, we often had much the best sessions when we afterwards adjourned to the pub and over a pint and a cigarette tongues would really begin to wag. It was two way traffic for I learned so much from them about all sorts of things. Indeed, overall we – my fellow tutors and I – may not have pushed back the frontiers of knowledge very far but we always hoped we had nourished curiosity, planted some seeds to thought, some itch to challenge political generalisations, some personal pleasure from reading and study.

We four tutors were pretty tired by the time the season was over and our work adjourned for the summer months. We were paid only the fees we earned from our teaching programmes which, shared out between us, amounted to the grand total of £180 each – and most of that was already mortgaged to cover advances we had received from the WEA for our living expenses through the winter. But what to do until next autumn? My own solution was to go back to Oxford and get myself accepted as a visiting speaker to the educational activities laid on by the Services. There was a huge appetite for information or informed speculation about plans being drafted for life in the post-war world. The possibilities seemed endless, the determination that things should be different irresistible. But it was in the Northamptonshire villages that the students and I got down to the nitty-gritty and really tried between us to work out what was possible and how it was to be done. When the war was over, I left the county and went on to other things but adult education had laid its hand upon me and what I did subsequently was always closely related to it. I have never lost my belief that it has an enormous contribution to make to our society.

Mary Turner 1921-1989

Mary wrote this account in 1989. It was originally published in North West district's pamphlet, WEA Voices: a Collection of Students' Writings.

It was strange how it all began. A friend brought me the University Extra Mural brochure, back in 1969, and the first class I attended – on human genetics – was, I think, run by the WEA. I was hooked, and went on to get an Extra Mural certificate (in history), for which I was required to attend sixty classes in not less than two years. I attended about 150 in five and a half years and produced a History of Collyhurst, Manchester.

During this period I met Mrs. Oddy, our Manchester branch registration secretary. Not one to miss a trick, she invited me to join the local branch and be on the committee. For some reason I thought I had better agree, and I am still on it.

I'm no good at committee work; very much a lone operator. My deafness handicapped me too. But this committee opened a door which I hadn't even thought of giving a shove with my foot. In March 1976 I was at a committee meeting when there was the usual brow-furrowing about what to offer the following winter. Without previous design on my part, I swear, I found myself quavering, 'I could do a few classes on the History of Collyhurst, if you think anybody'd be interested.' A few days later, appreciating that shortage of money is a permanent WEA problem, I even offered to do these classes for nothing, to assuage my guilt as an untried tutor as much as anything, I suspect. I worked full time and had enough to live on anyway, so the money was not important. Midsummer saw the arrival of an offer that I should take ten classes. I was alarmed. TEN classes? Good Lord! I'd never manage it. However, I don't give up easily, so mind was put to the situation. I knew the class would appear in the brochure, but realised extra advertising was essential in the educational desert that north Manchester seemed to be. There had to be personal spadework. Two hundred copies of what I hoped was an interesting ad. were put in the top box of my motor bike and I went round Collyhurst, Moston and Harpurhey for three weekends, shoving them through factory doors, house doors, shop doors and putting them on pub counters accompanied with conversation with landlords. I sent one to the *Manchester Evening News* and others to sundry broadcasters.

October arrived. By this time I felt a mixture of apprehension and surging adrenaline. Forty people came, from far and wide, delighted to find that 'their' Collyhurst actually had a history. It was December before I was able to sleep on Tuesday nights; the stimulation of the class was so great. That first series, which extended by request from the students to a further ten weeks after Christmas, I will never forget; the warmth, kindness, interest, feedback and generosity still give pleasure. In the years since my own research has continued and new topics have become available for teaching. I dread the arrival of the time when I'm too old or unfit to continue.

There's another side to all of this. Each of us has to do the best with what we've got – or to choose not to. I was withdrawn at fourteen from Grammar School because my guardian, my aunt, said they thought I wasn't trying, and my handwriting was very bad. Though herself a retired teacher, it didn't seem to occur to her or to my own teachers that I was as deaf as I really was, and that three family deaths in five months when I was thirteen had affected me. I worked in a cotton warehouse for a year and was then sent to commercial school – a very good one – which cost one pound per week. I had to shape because money wasn't flush. In three months I had certificates for 60 wpm, typing and 100 shorthand. Night school followed for improvement, and I soon got a job.

I'd always been a reader and a learner, but the Extra Mural Department and the WEA came into my life at the right time for me, when I knew my marriage was on the rocks and I wanted to do something for myself, something of headwork rather than what was offered at the time by the LEA locally. What I have had from adult education is more than fair exchange for a rocky married life, believe me. Have I changed? Undoubtedly. Coming from a family of teachers, I had always felt teaching was one thing I couldn't do, not even teaching somebody to type. And I was sure I couldn't put things over. That first huge Collyhurst class taught me otherwise.

Over the years perhaps a thousand people have actually joined my classes, and I also give talks to women's clubs, civic societies, local history societies and so on, throughout Greater Manchester, giving the WEA a plug as I go.

Teaching was a completely new skill for me but I have learned too that the power it confers has to be used carefully if it is to work properly. There are differences between groups – those in north Manchester are very different from, shall we say, a church ladies' group in Wilmslow! In both, though, a certain humour works. There are shy ones (and they are mostly men) who can be drawn out, perhaps before or after class but must be left alone during it. There's the occasional soap-boxer who has to be nudged a bit this way and that. And in north Manchester I've learned the wisdom of occasionally letting them all spark off each other for a few minutes and then calling them to order with a threat of fifty lines or being kept in! Ideas burgeon in such circumstances, and it's good.

I never thought it would be like this, you know. At first I wondered if there would always be a clevershins who would be able to outdo me but it hasn't happened so far, probably because I make it clear that I don't know it all myself. Often class members have been able to give new angles from their own experience so that we've all profited and nobody is downgraded.

With perhaps twenty or thirty exceptions, the last eleven years have been a sea of anonymous faces which yet were friends, and still are when a bit of help is needed. On the telephone somebody says, 'You won't remember me but I was in your class ...', and the voice at least rings a bell. And I help if I can.

My own learning never stops, nor should it if we are to heed Tawney's words:

'The purpose of the Association is to provide for men and women who want to take their bearings on the world, opportunities of co-operative study, in congenial company, with a teacher who knows enough of his business to be not only a teacher but a fellow-student ...'

I'm still a student myself, attending not only weekend courses but summer schools at Cambridge and Oxford for fourteen years now, the bonus at Oxford being that their methods are as flexible as those I appreciate in the WEA.

I attend nearly every meeting of my branch and go to the training days held by the district. I have something to give, but there's always something to learn and I like renewing contact with old friends and meeting new tutors. The WEA has forced me to realise that I have better skills than I was ever aware of, and I strive hard to pass on to others what it has done for me. If there were a view that I wish most earnestly we in the WEA could get over very strongly, it would be that there is more in each of us than we know, and that achieving deep satisfaction as individuals is actually a great deal easier than many will imagine.

There's also a strengthening feeling that one can put back into society what has been given to us. It's very much a two-way process, and as I get older I realise that the biblical expression 'casting bread upon the water' is true when it promises a greater return after many days. In terms of interest on investment, the WEA does a lot better than the stock market

Brenda Harold

Brenda wrote this account for the WEA Women's History Project in 2003.

Botany and genetics, the subjects that I tutor, are an unusual combination but they actually complement each other very well. After all, genetics began with Mendel's experiments on pea plants in the monastery garden.

I knew from a young age that I wanted to be a scientist and I had always loved plants. I grew seeds and pressed flowers when I was quite small, but I grew up in London only rarely visiting the country and the idea of becoming a biologist didn't cross my mind. I decided that pharmacy would be a good career but this required one biological subject at 'A' level. My school only offered botany and zoology as separate subjects and recommended that I took zoology. This was the moment when I recognised my passion for plants. I decided that if I couldn't take botany without zoology then I would have to take them both. Within a few weeks I knew that I had made the right decision and went on to take a degree in botany. At that time, in the early '60s, genetics was also becoming very exciting as the genetic code was being cracked. I therefore opted for the Botany Department at University College London where the main research interest was in genetics. I stayed there for six very happy years, following the BSc with a PhD on the genetics of a group of common wild flowers: cinquefoil and its relatives.

Marriage followed, and a job as assistant lecturer at one of the London colleges. This was the second major turning point in my career. I didn't expect to be good at teaching and was frankly terrified of my first lectures. I thought that it was necessary to be an extrovert and something of a showman, which I definitely am not. I quickly discovered that what matters is not the lecturer's performance but how much the students learn, and that I had a gift for explaining complex subjects in a comprehensible way. The students liked my lectures and I found that teaching was immensely rewarding. Within just a few weeks my ambition turned from research to becoming a senior tutor, which combines lecturing with pastoral care and the management of a teaching department.

Five years later our first baby arrived and I took a career break which actually proved to be a period of great personal development. I think that anyone who can get two small children round a supermarket without causing mayhem has highly developed negotiating skills and could handle the most difficult colleague in an employment situation. It should be possible to write this on one's CV but, sadly, prospective employers would not appreciate it. Since I intended to return to work later I looked for part-time jobs to keep my brain ticking over. These included my first experience of the WEA. The course was on genetics and it closed prematurely due to lack of students! In those days, the mid-'70s, genetics was still a very academic subject and had not hit the headlines. What I gained from that failed course was an understanding of just how much science a lay audience can absorb.

As soon as our children were at school I returned to a full-time lecturing job and the next twelve years or so were the battle that all working mothers understand. I felt squeezed between the family I loved and the job I loved, with no time for anything else. Eventually, though, the girls became independent and, close to my 50th birthday, I was promoted to senior tutor and deputy head of department.

So where does the WEA come in? Unfortunately, by the early '90s the university environment had changed. Student numbers soared and we went through modularisation, semesterisation and then into the Teaching Quality Assessment. This would have been fine had it meant a real increase in the emphasis on good teaching but, at the same time, the academic staff were being urged to produce more research. I decided to leave before the pressure actually made me ill, but with many regrets. Apart from missing the students and my colleagues I felt that I was failing the cause of women in academia. Although equal numbers of men and women embark on academic careers, very few women reach senior positions and this is especially striking in biology because it is generally regarded as a girls' subject. Having finally reached a senior position I was giving up. There was another factor in my decision, however, which was the still unfulfilled ambition to become a good field botanist.

There is no quick route to becoming a good botanist, or any other kind of naturalist. It means spending time in the field and poring through reference books. I started taking photographs of flowers and writing the names on them in order to learn them. Then I switched to slides so that I could illustrate talks and classes. Many of our wild plants are under threat but very few people these days are able to identify them, so this appeared to be a market niche. Since starting in 1998 I have tutored about 20 botanical courses ranging from 5 to 20 classes in length at many different WEA branches, and the order book is still full. Showing the wonders of nature to enthusiastic adult students is a great delight and some of the students will proceed to help environmental conservation in their own areas. Initially I didn't intend to offer courses on genetics but it became apparent that there was a demand as people became confused and alarmed by stories about GM crops, designer babies, human clones and so on. 'Genes Are Us' was a response to this and I was absolutely thrilled to receive a NIACE Adult Tutors Award for it, on the recommendation of my students, which made it even better.

So I'm now working on my final ambitions, to improve the public understanding of science and, in particular, to encourage the conservation of our local flora. This is sufficient for a whole lifetime, but many botanists continue working into a ripe old age!

The Organisers

It was a very busy life for, besides the programme of classes, I had often to speak at Saturday conferences run by the Co-op and similar organisations. Sometimes we would try to get a new branch going by descending on a village with handbills and seeking interviews with the school teacher, the vicar and anyone else we were told might be helpful.

Janet Cockerill, 1940s

In 1982 the district secretary asked me to be responsible for women's studies in the East Midland district. Needless to say, it was a position with a soupcon of honour and glory, but no financial reward. I simply got to attend lots of evening branch meetings to explain women's studies to one man and a dog. The considerable advantage I had when 'selling' fairly subversive women's courses to both small and large branches was that I looked like a respectable, middle-class, middle-aged lady, rather than the stereotypical 'women's libber'. So the reaction of conservatively-inclined branch members tended to be, 'If Marjorie says it's OK, it must be OK.'

Marjorie Calow, 1980s

The first step was to identify places where people actually go; schools seemed the obvious places to begin. Contacts were made with groups of parents in schools across Mexborough and Goldthorpe areas. Many of the schools were developing 'community' perspectives and were fairly welcoming. The response from parents was extremely positive and resulted in the formation of groups in seven schools and a further seven in other centres within the various localities. At the core of all this activity was the principle that the women themselves were able from the start to play a full role in deciding what the sessions should be about. Informing the process throughout was the aim not of simply running orthodox courses that might come and go, rather we sought a model whereby women could develop for themselves more holistic, long-term learning programmes and group activities rooted in their own agendas.

Trish Land, 1990s

The separate role of organising tutor, later tutor organiser, began to be discussed in the WEA after the First World War. The organisation was seen to have the potential for growth beyond the capacity of the voluntary membership to capture new students. It was suggested that the skills, techniques and approaches of WEA volunteers could be taken further by people with more time to work at recruiting students. The first group of paid organisers were supported by a grant from the Cassell Trust in 1919 and included one woman, Sophie Green. It was, however, a long time before organisers became a standard component in the districts: a handful were paid for from special funds throughout the twenties and thirties.

Organising tasks remained largely distributed between the voluntary members and the district secretary. Entrepreneurial district secretaries, such as Frank Jacques in Eastern district, persuaded young women graduates during the war to work as tutor organisers, whilst only receiving the fees for their teaching. This was not a model that could work indefinitely and was opposed after the war by the Tutors' Association. The period after the Second World War saw a great expansion of university extra mural staff tutors, allocated to relatively small geographical areas, who worked closely with the WEA, and created a wider precedent of professional class organising. In 1973 the Russell report, with its emphasis on developing education for groups of 'disadvantaged' adults, was a spur to WEA districts to appoint tutor organisers. Government funding for trade union education from 1975, available as part of the Social Contract, introduced a further encouragement to develop tutor organisers with specialist roles. Since the '80s the exploitation of funding from waves of government regional regeneration schemes, from Europe and charities have created a mass of new organising jobs, often part-time and always temporary, which women have largely taken.

The job of organising for the WEA in the early days was focussed on the development of new branches and within these new classes. Today it has become a mix of finance, diplomacy and curriculum management with mundane administration and housekeeping. Low key but persistent contact with groups of students, volunteers and potential students and volunteers, is interspersed with the daily routine of publicity production and distribution, travel, the arranging of rooms and tutors and yet more travel. The traditional links to the Labour movement now extend to maintaining partnerships with a huge range of organisations. Tutor recruitment and support is continuous. When the role was relatively new it carried some of the power of the established Labour movement in partnership with the universities, and all the status that bestowed – a role naturally occupied by men. With changes in funding, the kinds of classes to be organised and a massive increase in provision, the job lost its glamour and gained a mountain of paperwork.

The expansion of women's employment in the WEA, in the last two decades, is characterized by temporary organising posts, often carrying new names, often part-time. There were equal numbers of female and male organisers for the first time in the early 1990s and women had begun to creep into the majority by the mid '90s. Here are some stories from the organisers.

WOMEN'S SECTIONS IN THE W.E.A.

The need for women's education has been looked at for a moment. It would be well to consider now the question of the formation of special women's sections and committees in the W.E.A. Of course, such sections and committees would always be responsible to the branch council, so that the solidarity of the branch and the close co-operation of men and women would be thoroughly ensured.

The reasons for having women's sections may be said to be as follows:

1. Women's sections are desirable in that they can take into special account the needs of their members, both as regards subject and time. Though, needless to say, it is an excellent thing when men and women can study side by side, women are often interested in subjects that do not appeal to men; or it may happen, especially in the case of married women, that they can most conveniently meet at an hour that would not suit their men-folk.

2. Women's sections can give valuable help in the way of collecting information for the branch on such matters as wages and housing, and on the work of Care Committees in the district.

3. It has been found that the more retiring women are far readier to give an opinion or to take part in a discussion when the committee or class is composed entirely of members of their own sex.

4. Lastly, women's sections can do much missionary work, both in the way of approaching organisations and individual women. They will be able to devise means to attract the people whom we want so badly in the W.E.A. —the people who perhaps bring no book-learning with ... but something that we want far more, and s... ...

Sophie Green 1886-c1960

This account was written by Bob Chapman, tutor organiser for Northamptonshire, for the occasion of the presentation of a photograph of Sophie to Kettering Centre for the Unemployed in 2001.

Sophie Green, pioneering figure in women's education between the wars, was WEA tutor and organiser in Kettering from 1919–39. Her appointment in Kettering came at a time when major efforts were being made to establish provision of adult education outside the metropolitan areas. When the Cassell Trust offered to fund the appointment of five tutor organisers in selected areas, and Kettering and district was one of those areas, Sophie was appointed to the post, which she held for the next twenty years.

Sophie Green was the protégée of Helen Stocks, an influential Oxford tutor who had taught university classes in Kettering and who had noted the potential of her young student, at that time employed in the local Co-op clothing factory. Sophie caught the attention of her tutor because she was enthusiastic, committed and intelligent – and highly regarded amongst her fellow workers.

Although she lacked formal qualifications – a blight, she always felt, to her academic aspirations – she had the intelligence and charisma to make things happen. Appointed to the position in November 1919, a decision influenced by Helen Stocks' vigorous support, Sophie's first role was to return to the very clothing factory that she had just left to tutor a course in English literature to her erstwhile friends and fellow workers.

Limited as a tutor by her lack of formal education, Sophie attended tutor training classes, many summer schools and, later, Bryn Mawr College in Pennsylvania, in an attempt to gain for herself the education that her schooling had not offered. In many ways, it was Sophie's 'disadvantaged' background which gave her empathy with working-class woman in Kettering. Her student-centred

approach and her unstinting willingness to help individuals, running tutorials and study groups in her own home to prepare for the next term's courses, made her much loved among her students.

In the early 1920s, several of her factory-worker students spent a term in residence at Girton and Newnham Colleges, Cambridge – a culture shock for all concerned – and a regular pattern of residence at Newnham summer schools was established. Sophie was driven by the determination to offer to others the educational opportunities that she herself had been denied. She was a motivating tutor and a far-sighted organiser. George Chester, who later became general secretary of the Boot and Shoe Operatives Union, described her as 'sympathetic, studious, and not afraid of hard grinding work... displaying a vision which few people reach.'

There was a general outcry when Sophie Green resigned in November 1939, for she was much loved and valued. There were many reasons for her departure, not least the strain of organising classes during wartime and the responsibilities of having two evacuees billeted with her. Her last report gives an indication of her work – constant activity or waiting for buses – its tone reflecting the words of George Pateman, her first district secretary, '... organising comes out badly on paper.'

> 'Besides the places where I held classes, I gave single lectures at Ringstead, Raunds, Burton Latimer, Loddington, Chelveston, Corby, Oakley, Higham, Castle Ashby, Rothwell and for several organisations in Kettering. I have spent a good deal of time in my work on the local Education Committee. I have been chairman of one of the sub-committees and a governor of one of the C of E schools.
>
> I have given freely of my time to further WEA interests and to help WEA members. A good deal of this useful work cannot be fully explained in a report. It should, I feel be noted, that a great deal of my time is spent in travelling and waiting about for buses. For instance it takes 3_ hours travelling to and from Ringstead – a journey that by car would be completed in 45 minutes.'

Grace Colman 1892-1971

This account, by Zoë Munby, is based on the Dictionary of Labour Biography, *Vol. 3; WEA* London district Annual Reports *and the records of London University.*

Grace was a clergyman's daughter, born in London and growing up near Leeds. She won a scholarship to Newnham College, Cambridge, where she studied history and economics and during this period joined the Labour Party. After university she worked as a tutorial class tutor and at Ruskin College from 1920-25. In 1925 she was appointed as staff tutor for tutorial classes at London University where she worked until 1940. Her teaching consisted mainly of tutorial classes in economics, with a regular number of day and weekend schools for the London WEA Women's Committee, for the TUC and WEA branches. She was an individual subscriber to the WEA. Towards the end of the '30s the subjects of her short courses and day schools, in line with many WEA tutors, tended to be the international situation, re-armament and colonial issues. She wrote two booklets published as student texts by the WEA, *Capitalist Combines* and *The Structure of Modern Industry*.

London had been one of the earliest of the WEA districts to establish a women's committee, in 1909. There are reports of its work up to 1915, and again from 1919 to '21; it was re-established in 1925/6. In the earlier periods the committee was concerned with work with the Women's Co-op Guild and courses for young women's organisations, shop workers, mothers' meetings, church groups and those courses which would attract women in the home and young single women. The London Women's Committee re-launched in 1925 was a grouping of affiliated Labour movement women's organisations. Barbara Wootton, then teaching WEA classes for London University Extra Mural Department in the evenings and working for the joint research department of the Labour Party and Trades Union Congress during the day, convened the first meeting and Margaret Bondfield, trade unionist and Labour MP spoke. The work of the committee became focussed on providing education for women trade unionists, women in the Labour Party and the Women's Co-op Guild. Grace was appointed as organiser for the London WEA Women's Committee in 1926, a post that carried a salary, although by 1929/30 she is described as holding this position in an honorary capacity. She dramatically increased

the work of the committee, leading in the following year to an additional appointment of a part-time lecturer for the women's committee. In 1927/8 Grace developed what was possibly the WEA's first venture into teacher training.

> 'Arising out of the work of the women's committee and the need for tutors for pioneer work generally, Miss G.M.Colman arranged a course of thirteen fortnightly meetings for a training group in methods of teaching. Ten students attended and the work included the preparation of syllabuses, the delivery of lectures and the use of illustrations. In addition the group has done valuable work in collecting photographs and designing charts for use in lectures and short courses arranged by the committee. Such a course indicates one method whereby some of our students and other people new to our work may be introduced to methods of teaching to fit them for tackling courses of a pioneer character.'

WEA London Bulletin, 1937/8

By the following year Grace's training group was an established feature of the women's programme. They raised funds to buy materials and compiled sets of resources for classes which were loaned out to tutors and were regularly up-dated over the following years. The scale of the work of women's committees such as this is invisible in the formal lists of WEA classes, as only grant earning courses were listed, along with the more prestigious day and weekend schools. In 1933/4 the London WEA Women's Committee provided 160 single lectures in addition to the nine short courses recorded in the *Annual Report*, all bar one taught by women and *all* given by volunteers. In 1937/8 Grace ran speakers' classes for members of the Women's Education Committee, although the work of the committee was declining from this period. She resigned from her organising role in 1936, owing to pressure of other work. She took up the reins again as secretary in 1939, on the resignation of Miss L.Chamberlain, although the committee appears to have disappeared soon after the outbreak of war.

During the 1930s she had become increasingly involved with the Labour Party's programme of schools for women members and taught at these all over the country.

'Grace had the ability, which not many lecturers have, of making most complex political issues clear to hundreds of women, who for the most part had little formal education beyond elementary school. Although an academic herself, she was so simple in her approach to life generally, and in her style of lecturing she not only won the confidence of her eager students but gave *them* confidence to express themselves and demonstrate that they really did understand so many issues, which at first sight appeared so complex. There are today in the northern counties in particular, very many women in public life, who would be the first to acknowledge that they owe a great debt of gratitude to their unpaid tutor.'

Sara Barker, quoted in the *Dictionary of Labour Biography*

She was widely active in Labour and women's organisation. From 1932 she was a representative on the Standing Joint Committee of Industrial Women's Organisations which she chaired in 1938. She was active in the London Co-operative Society, the Co-operative Party, the Women's Co-operative Guild and the London Labour Party Women's Advisory Committee.

Grace's activism extended beyond work with women. In 1925 she joined, and remained active within, the General and Municipal Workers' Union and played an active role in the 1926 General Strike, working with the Nottingham Trades Council. During the '30s she was a magistrate; a temporary civil servant during the war and an ARP warden.

She stood for parliament in 1929, 1931, and 1935 and was elected for Tynemouth in 1945. She lost her parliamentary seat in 1951, in part due to a boundary change. She continued with a variety of paid and unpaid jobs for the Labour Party, active in the Women's Co-op Guild, the Northumberland Women's Advisory Committee and the RSPCA. She remained intellectually active to the end. Unable to walk and in a North Shields nursing home, she was working on research into the situation of old people and the supply of nursing homes at the time of her death, aged seventy-nine.

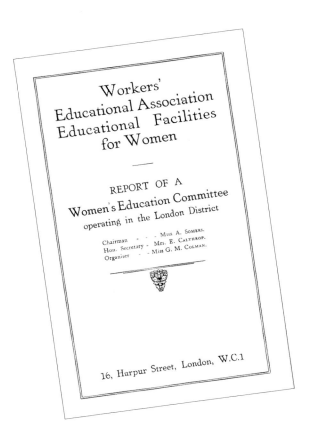

Jean McCrindle

These extracts are taken from an interview with Jean by Zoë Munby, in 2003, for the WEA Women's History Project. Jean grew up in London and studied history at St. Andrews University. She was appointed as tutor organiser in 1960 for the West of Scotland district of the WEA, as a twenty-two year-old. She left the WEA in 1963 for a post at the Extra Mural Department of the University of Ghana, as a tutor organiser for women and co-operatives. After two years she returned and worked for six months in London as a probation officer. In the mid-'60s she co-edited a journal of political debate, in Rome. She returned to have her first child and work teaching women's studies and current affairs courses at art colleges, in Sheffield, then in London. She was involved with the early feminist movement and campaigns. In 1978 she co-edited, with Sheila Rowbotham, Dutiful Daughters, a book of interviews with women. In 1979 she became lecturer in Political Thought and Women's Studies at the newly opened Northern College for adult residential education, in Barnsley. She worked there until the early nineties and was treasurer of the national Women Against Pit Closures group. Since retirement Jean has completed a PhD and is currently writing a libretto for an opera on women's involvement in the miners' strike.

I thought, are there any women? I'd begun teaching international relations in the evenings in Lanarkshire and in the first groups there were a couple of women that came to those classes. They must have been desperate: they were living in Motherwell, hardly anyone had any television and there was no cinema. Social life must have been quite extraordinarily restrictive. They came to my classes. I think because it was quite unusual to have a woman tutor and I got to know them quite well. They were young women, not much older than me, with young children. They were absolutely faithful students. I started to say to them, 'Well look, why don't we try and get a class going in the afternoons for you and you can bring your friends?' I would say, 'Why can't you bring more friends?' 'Well, their husbands won't let them out.' Or, 'No one is going to be able to baby sit.' Or, 'What about the husband?' 'Oh, they won't baby sit.' So I think that was where I originally got the idea.

I called a meeting, in Motherwell, using these two or three contacts I had made, they brought with them their friends and the children. I put it to them that we could do this class on the position of women in society and they were all really keen. I said, 'But we've got to find somewhere for the children, we've got to have a crèche for the children.' So I went to the medical officer for health in Lanarkshire. Apparently you had to do that in those days because you couldn't have children looked after in unregulated crèches. Nurseries were deeply frowned on so only people with desperate circumstances would ever put their children in a nursery. I was only 22 and he must have thought who the hell is this? I said, 'I want to have a crèche, I want to find premises where women can come and the children can be in the crèche.' He said, 'That's impossible, it's illegal, you can't.' So I went to see the Women's Voluntary Service and I said, 'Would you provide a crèche for women who have got children?' 'Oh yes, we would love to do that.' We just ignored him; he never came and took us to court.

I had read Simone de Beauvoir in my last year at university, which was 1959. I had read *The Second Sex*. It must have come out in France a couple of years before it came out in England. One male friend who was an absolute addict of everything going on in Paris, like Sartre, had recommended it to me and from then on I thought right, that's fine, I'm a feminist, I'm a de Beauvoirite. I think I actually referred in one article to a group as the de Beauvoirites of Lanarkshire. No way would anyone in Scotland acknowledge that! But I taught de Beauvoir in the classes, when I got the women to come, and they loved it. Some of them read it and we discussed it. They went away and wrote stuff on it. They took it back into their homes, they discussed it with their husbands and so on. It was like a kind of early intimation that 'ordinary women' who weren't particularly political, as I was, were interested in this. Not that anyone at that time in politics, that I was involved with, was particularly interested in the position of women. I don't know where I got that from - something clicked.

I remember the inspector of the classes of adult education, a woman, sitting at the back of one of the classes and she got really keen on the ideas and started discussing. I think she was quite pleased. The students were in their late 20s, early 30s, with children under five, a couple were older, but mainly they were stuck at home. It was very difficult to find jobs at that time; anyway the whole ethos was that you stayed with the children until they were ready to go to school. There were one or two books being produced, looking at the question of women, working women - Pearl Jephcott and Hannah Gavron's wonderful book called Captive Wives. These must have been all published in the '50s. Hannah Gavron's book looked at how distressed women were feeling at being stuck at home, after the war. I gathered the few books that there were. I used de Beauvoir's chapters in The Second Sex, but with English/Scottish examples and it just went like a bomb. I did something on psychoanalysis and women - it must have been Freud - and something on women at work.

I taught quite traditionally, I think. We weren't yet into the period when the class decided the curriculum. I decided the curriculum, and they went with me. That was what I had been taught to do, I

introduced the topic, prepared it beforehand, produced some handouts and then we discussed it. I think they were bursting to talk. They were wonderful, it was really moving. None of these women were having the ideas they wanted to have. They weren't living the lives they really wanted to live. They knew that. Their husbands were incredibly supportive. I remember them coming to me, two or three weeks into the courses, and saying, 'My husband says I've changed completely since I've come to this class.' It was before the women's movement. It must have been going on all over the country, I suppose, women feeling that way. You feel the movement coming but you don't know what was going to come.

Chris Aldred

Chris was interviewed in 2002 for WEA Scotland's Centenary Celebrations. She moved to Aberdeen in 1971, on finishing university, and was involved in a women's liberation group there, setting up a women's studies course with the university extramural department, in 1973, at the same time as the first Aberdeen WEA women's rights course was being planned. In autumn 1975 she became the North of Scotland's only tutor organiser, working closely with Margaret Marshall, who became district secretary in 1977. Together they pioneered work in WEA women's education in a number of areas, and constituted the only all-female district staff team for a number of years. Chris was acting district secretary for a period. She moved in 1990 to a post at Aberdeen College, teaching psychology, and then worked in community outreach for the college. She is currently Adult Learning Development Officer with Aberdeen City Council.

When I started as tutor organiser I chose to do social purpose education and trade union education. The Scottish TUC opened its college at Treesbank. I can't quite remember how it came about, but there was a suggestion that perhaps there should be a course for women offered...as one of the only people who was prepared to jump up and down and say, 'I can do that', I said 'I can do that.' I planned out a Monday to Friday course for women trade unionists and wrote the materials and found that was a really great experience. I ran about three of those courses and

worked with women who were involved in the Lee Jeans occupation later on, which was a work-in at a factory in the South West of Scotland, and met all sorts of people who were very interesting. The content of that course is quite staid when looking at it today. It was about how you take part in your trade union, how you become a trade union representative as a woman, what health and safety issues there were for women, women's rights, and so on. It was really a standard course but it was quite a mind changing, feelings changing, experience for the women involved. For the first time it was taken as read that women were trade unionists, that women had the right to a voice in a trade union, that we had issues which were legitimate for trade unions to consider. That there wasn't such a thing as a women's issue and a trade union issue....

The WEA had a liaison committee on trade union education and it had representation from the professional staff trade union in the WEA, which at that time was ASTMS and we had a special section called 'WES', which was the Workers' Education Section. I'd become quite active in WES.... When the trade union rep. on the WEA's trade union committee said that there was the prospect of writing a series of books and that members would be approached to see if anyone was interested in writing anything, I said, 'Is anyone interested in writing anything about women?' Nobody had really bagged that area so I said, 'I'll do that.'....

It was intended to be a contribution to the debate about what trade union education was. In the WEA there was a lot of involvement by male trade union education tutors, who saw trade union education really as the cutting edge of social change but didn't really see women's education or women trade unionists as having a very critical role in that. So my determination to write it stemmed from trying to make sure that that it was balanced. The women who I'd worked with made me think that there was a need for some sort of book that set out the arguments...

We had a specific branch for women's studies and that caused no end of local fuss, as you can imagine. The Aberdeen branch said, 'Well, you could quite easily do that work under our auspices, we would welcome you in', and we said, 'No we want to do it our way.' The women in the group were very determined to keep that going. There were parallel squabbles all over the WEA: you could have a specialist trade union studies branch, which all these kind of, trade unionist, cutting edge, people were saying was the important way to engage a new section of the voluntary movement. We also had a legitimate argument in saying that a women's studies branch could be needed. Because the women's studies branch had such an influence on the development of the district what then happened was that the branch itself withered away as the members were sucked into district activities and became tutors, and developed all sorts of projects and ideas.

The women's work grew I suppose from a range of women's courses.... We began to think about the way we were setting up those courses and decided that actually what we needed was something that was going to be more relevant to women in communities. I suppose that by the late '70s we also had funding from the then job creation scheme. We used it to set up crèches, as one of the projects, and by setting up crèches we were able to reach what we saw as the very important target group of working class women in communities, with young children. They were the main educational under achievers as we saw them. Those courses were about trying to find what people wanted to study, to examine their own lives, to start where they were and I suppose they were the beginning of a whole tradition of work that's carried on in the north of Scotland from then 'til now....

The Women's Education Advisory Committee was set up at national level to look at promoting developments in women's education. There had been a huge fight over whether it should be called 'The Women's Education' or 'The Women's Studies' advisory committee. In Aberdeen we were very much on the side of it being 'The Women's Education Advisory Committee' because we didn't want to be associated exclusively with the strand of academic women's studies education. So, my participation in the Women's Advisory Committee maybe started with the fact that I was one of the people who were shouting that it should be 'education'. It was about the kind of thing that I suppose we would now refer to as personal development education, it was about encouraging women to become everything they could be, not just to learn about woman as an academic subject choice.

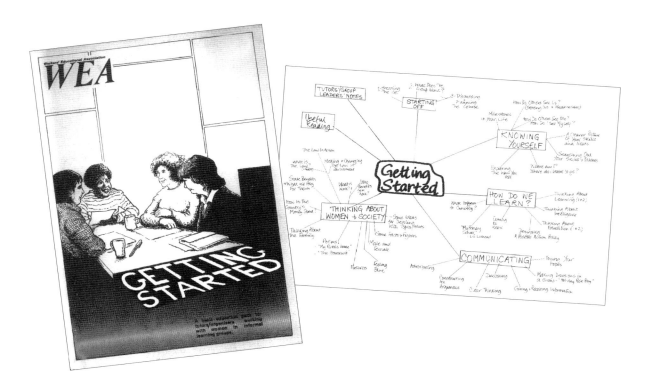

Kath Locke 1928-1992

This account was complied by Zoë Munby, drawing on WEA records; obituaries; the video, We Are Born To Survive, (Kath Locke Educational Trust); with help from WEA North West district staff, Jackie Ould, Norma Turner, and the Armed Iqubal Ullah Centre - Race Relations Archive, Manchester.

Kath was born in 1928 in Manchester, moving when she was five to Blackpool. The bullying and tormenting she experienced as a black child at school in what was then a very white town gave her an early understanding of prejudice. The African names which she, her brothers and sisters had, were rejected as heathen at their schools. Her father, a Nigerian seaman married to a white woman, encouraged his children to see themselves as African, rather than English, an identity Kath retained for life. Prejudice followed her into the family where Kath and her brothers and sisters were treated as an embarrassment to her white extended family.

Kath was back living in Manchester by her teens and politically involved. By the 1950s she was a single parent of three children, concerned about issues around play and childcare which drew her towards community politics. By the '70s she was working as a hospital domestic and was active in NUPE. Living in the Crescents in Hulme she played an active part in the campaigns around the redevelopment of Hulme and Moss Side, starting a local magazine *Alcatraz* and organising tenants in direct action – including one demonstration when they threw bugs into a council meeting.

The Civil Rights movement in America of the '60s had a profound influence on her. She had met some of the people who had attended the Pan African Congress in Manchester in 1945 and was to campaign for a plaque to be erected on the building where it had been held. She was involved in the '60s with founding a branch of the Universal Coloured People's Organisation in Manchester and experienced the demonstrations of the '60s.

Kath's awareness of the importance of developing a black identity led her to work with other women in the Black Women's Mutual Aid to support black children. They campaigned for schools to develop an awareness of the issues for black children and for the introduction of black history and culture into schools. They ran Saturday and summer schools. She took up invitations to speak to African students at the university and developed a scheme whereby African students were matched with a black family with teenage children. She saw the benefits for the student of developing an understanding of black English society, and the benefits for the children of having a role model and a view of university and the wider world it offered. The Black Women's Mutual Aid evolved into the Manchester Black Women's Co-operative and, in 1979, separated to form Abasindi.

Abasindi broke away to establish itself as a women's run co-operative and funded itself by crafts, dressmaking, hair plaiting – refusing to take state aid so they could remain independent. This independence was significant in 1981. Abasindi responded to the New Cross fire, which resulted in the deaths of 13 young black people, by organising an enormous contingent to join the London demonstration. Some months later, when Moss Side youth rioted in response to growing tensions with police, Abasindi were able to establish immediate support. Kath, with Abasindi, fought a number of successful deportation campaigns and as an individual frequently supported individuals experiencing racial injustice. A socialist and feminist, Kath always saw herself as a black person first, a woman and working class afterwards.

In 1978 Kath finished a Youth and Community workers' course at Manchester Polytechnic, during which she had researched the history of community struggles in Moss Side and establish a black students' forum. She began working as a development officer with the Trade Union and Basic Education (TUBE) project of the North West district of the WEA in about 1980. TUBE worked with many of the black organisations in Manchester, such as the West Indian Centre and the Black Parents' Movement. They ran courses on African and Caribbean history, a 'Black Studies' course, and a Yoroba language course, in addition to courses for the Asian community. In the area of rights and community politics they organised courses on immigration and nationality law, sickle cell anaemia, black workers and trade unions courses and a range of anti-racist programmes and training, mainly for white people.

Kath saw education as a way of overcoming the disadvantages experienced in a racist society and saw TUBE's role as providing a kind of community forum. She was a facilitator, co-tutor and development worker. She died a year after her retirement from the WEA.

Rehana Mohamed

This account is an extract from an interview with Zoë Munby for the WEA Women's History Project in 2002.

I was born in Mombassa, in Kenya, in 1963. My grandfather had come to Kenya as a soldier in the British army; when my father was seven my grandfather brought him to Kenya, to live with him. My grandmother refused to travel on the sea and stayed behind in India with the daughters. In Kenya we had a second grandmother and my father had a good education. When he left school he was in the British police, in Kenya. My mother was born in Kenya and my uncles worked for British banks. My parents had an arranged marriage. I was the youngest of five children. I remember school in Kenya, we used a slate. There weren't enough slates to go round and if you had no slate you wrote on your leg with chalk. I remember music classes and trying out the instruments. Once we broke a guitar and six of us were punished, made to stand outside in the sun and say the 16 times table. I cried. But I still remember the 16 times table, even when I can't remember the other tables.

My mother wanted to see Pakistan and meet my father's mother. In 1947, during Partition, my grandmother and her three girls had travelled from India to Pakistan. My parents visited when they had just two children and mother loved Pakistan. Father bought land there and thought that this was a good place to educate his children. He always wanted us to have a good education. We made a second visit in 1971, when I was eight years old. My father built a house in Fasselebad and my oldest brother went to the Sacred Heart school there. My grandmother wanted us to live in the village. I was spoiled in Pakistan. I couldn't get a place at the Sacred Heart school, it was for boys; schools for girls were government public schools. The four of us were put back into classes for younger children because we couldn't read and write Urdu; we were in two classes, two together in each class.

My father didn't like Pakistan. He didn't like the way people did business, so he went back to Kenya. He worked in Mombassa and Nairobi with my uncles. In the next two years the rules for entry to Britain changed, you needed a visa. While my father was visiting us in Pakistan in 1973 the rules changed in Kenya and Asians were forced to leave. My father couldn't go back and he lost his business, he lost everything. He was only thirty-eight and he had a

breakdown, worrying day-by-day how he could save the situation. He had a heart attack and died the same day. We were left dependent on our grandparents. We had British passports, but no visas. My father had applied for a visa before he died and it arrived three days after he died. My mother wrote to the British embassy explaining that he was dead and eventually they released the visa to his eldest son. My brother was only fourteen but he had to go on his own to Britain.

My maternal grandparents and uncles had had to leave Kenya and go to Britain. They left with the clothes they stood up in. At the airport there were buckets of soapy water and they had to wash their hands to remove any rings. Their servants told them, 'Leave the keys with us.' My grandmother had been good to her servants, she had one per child. They said, 'Don't worry, we'll try to do something.' They did send some things back to them in England.

My brother went to England, to our maternal grandparents. He had to finish his education. It was a really hard time. My grandmother came over to Pakistan and brought my brother back to England. He had to work to support us in Pakistan. He worked in a factory and part-time with my uncle. My mother did sewing. The four of us remaining kept putting in applications for visas and kept getting rejected. My brother applied here in England for us and we got visas. I came to England when I was 16. I was too old to go to school. We got visas on the condition that we didn't take benefits. We all worked in factories, mother had to work – father had died too young for her to get a pension. We all got jobs in Rochdale. We wanted to get an education but there were no opportunities for classes. It was difficult for girls to go to classes, my uncles thought at that time that girls should not go. After a while my sister and I went to classes secretly. My brother started going too. The first class I did was in administration, when I was 17. It had always been my father's aim that we would be educated. Once you try education, you have a thirst, you are always trying.

My two sisters were married and I was expected to get married. It was a difficult time. I married in 1982 and had two children. I helped my husband with his business but I wanted a wage, so I went to work for Rochdale Council, as an interpreter, a receptionist, helping people fill in forms. I still did do some work for my husband.

When the children were five and six we moved to Pakistan: my husband's mother was ill and we wanted to see his parents. We also thought the children would get a good religious education there. We rented out the house and sold my husband's business. We were three and a half years in Pakistan. The children got on well with the Koran and I felt they'd catch up with their other education later. We lived in Multan city, two and a half hour's journey from the village. Then I heard that my mother had had a stroke and was in intensive care. I asked my husband – I really wanted to visit my mum and take the children.

It was hard coming back. There were problems with the house, it had been rented out to students. The children went back to school and I went as a volunteer helper in their school. My husband was still in Pakistan sorting out his business and I was on Income Support for three months. Then I worked as a support tutor. I heard about the WEA computer course and enrolled on it, in 1995. I always tried to be first in and last to leave, helping the tutor; I became a volunteer and got a Level 1 certificate. When the course finished I asked if I could help set up another course for Asian women. Towards the end of 1995 I started working as a tutor, teaching arts and crafts. I worked part-time for two years. I was introduced to the WEA by Lynda Howarth. She has been a great influence. She would say, 'How much work can you do?' And I'd say, 'As much as possible.' As well as part time tutoring I was taking part in courses to increase my qualifications, nine or ten courses. As soon as I knew I could work for the WEA I was always doing courses. I enrolled at Rochdale on evening classes and now I had support from the family, I could leave my children with my sisters in law. In 1999 the WEA got ESF and SRB funding for the Asian Women's Training Project and advertised a co-ordinator's post. At first I wasn't sure about applying, lots of people would apply. But I got an interview: Ian and Lynda and a member of the Asian community interviewed me – they wanted to check that they got someone with bilingual skills. I got the job and now I run a successful women's training project. I'm lucky: I'm in the WEA Women's Education Committee and have so many links. I see things as a volunteer – mine is a small project, but my links are wide. I'm on the Rochdale SRB Community Forum, I sit on the Community Chest Panel, I'm on the Executive of the SRB, I'm on the Education Policy Committee in North Western district of the WEA. The project is on going. This training project will be side-by-side with a new project for women's businesses.

My husband came back to England in 1992. My family is proud of me now. All of my nieces and nephews are very close and love to stay at my home. Asian women in Rochdale support our project and there are many exciting possibilities for the future.

WEA Guide to Classes with Childcare, 1982, published as a result of the work of the revived Women's Education Advisory Committee

Debra Walley

The organisation of this publication leaves some categories of WEA workers un-represented. Recent years have seen the steady growth of women who work in the WEA as crèche workers, family learning field workers, and different kinds of support workers. This account is an extract from an interview by Zoë Munby with Debra in 2003.

I was born in 1969 and grew up on the Miners' estate in Kidsgrove. It was lovely – kids and parents playing in the street. I loved all my schools; even school teachers and I did OK but not as well as I would have liked with my qualifications. I didn't want to get married, I was going to have loads of animals, adopt children and be a vet. I used to feed the hens with dad before I did a morning paper round, then an evening one. I worked in a pet shop and in an oatcake shop after school and on Saturdays. I met my husband in that oatcake shop, when I was fourteen. My dad supported us a lot with homework but I was a fool to myself. I just wanted to get out of school, get a job. I did YTS at Churchill's potbank in Sandyford. I stayed about twelve months and then during the Potters' Holidays I went for a job doing industrial sewing. After the holiday I went straight into that, did machining for three years. In those three years I had my daughter, when I was nineteen. I went back to work and my mother brought up my daughter.

Then I finished work and had a few years off. I moved to my new home with my husband. I had my son in 1994 and I began to take him to Meet-a-Mum and a playgroup. My friend was supervisor and she wanted me to be assistant supervisor. They asked, would I be prepared to do NVQ level 2? So I went once a week and got my certificates. Speaking to a mum who was doing a course with the WEA, she mentioned me to Sue, the tutor, who told Mary, the crèche organiser. Mary wanted to see me down at Whitfield Valley School, to do a crèche there, so that's how it came about: it was September 1998.

I knew Barbara Hill, who was also a tutor with the WEA, she was hoping to run an after school club down at Whitfield Valley. So I applied for the job, and did that for fifteen months. I still did WEA crèches, and the after school club. I've also been working with the WEA's Surestart projects for two years. I supply activities and equipment and go out to playgroups. Parents and children do things together. It's nice to see them working alongside one another. Because where we go, they don't have gluing, paints, play dough – they don't provide these things. It's just nice to give the children the opportunity to do them. There's a lot of thinking behind it: we plan the activities once a month and prepare the materials we need. You meet many different mums who perhaps need advice; you give them advice but also being careful of where you tread, respectful of their wishes.

With the crèches, it's nice to see the children growing up. If you have a half term break they come back and they're crawling, or walking. It's the ability of the children to develop their own personalities. I've had the experience of working with children from birth to fifteen-year-olds with the WEA. Working with other cultures can be hard: I have to be told two or three times how to pronounce names but the other crèche workers help me. They support you as you support them.

After I finished my NVQ I did British Sign Language for four years. I have used it. Not with carers but with children with hearing problems, I know how to communicate with them. I'm doing NVQ level 3 now, because we have to have it by 2004. I wanted to leave college alone after finishing sign language but the twelve months have flown and hopefully I'll be finished by May this year.

My mum has taught me a lot. She's always found ways of managing, during the strike, cooking when times are hard. Her brother's wife, June, had Parkinson's and mum wanted to do something, so she did. She has always done things – self defence, things like that. So she ran the Potteries Marathon to raise money for Parkinson's for three years. She did two years on her own and then last year we did it as a team. There was mum, myself, my friend, a father and daughter. We did it in memory of auntie June, who passed away last August. We collected over £3,000.

I go to my old neighbour Jack once a week and do his laundry; I've done it for five years, ever since his wife died. They were like nan and grandad to me, she taught me things, like all about baking. I want to concentrate on my daughter and son now. My husband has had diabetes for twenty years and he is due to go into hospital soon. He's had to give up work. I'm a carer for everyone in the house, animals and all. I did things all the wrong way round but I wouldn't be without my children for love nor money.

With the WEA I've been to lots of places, I've had support by being put through courses. I've met many people through working for the WEA. When you're out shopping you see them and have a good chinwag. You see the child growing up, or they've had another baby – just brilliant.

Women in the District Office

It was a small office consisting of two and a bit rooms with a shared toilet on the landing. I shared one room with the district secretary and the other room was occupied by two admin assistants and a finance officer. The 'bit' of a room was the kitchen/duplicator room.

We only had the basic tools to work with – manual typewriters, ink duplicator and a manual calculator but it seemed to cover our needs. All our course syllabuses were typed on stencils (skins) and stored in a cabinet in case we needed extra copies. The only problem we had with these was that corrections were not easily disguised and if you typed too hard the 'o's would drop out of the words. This was particularly a problem when I progressed to an electric typewriter. Accuracy was also very important in our work as the district secretary did not like any errors showing on the paperwork and when I had to type up agendas and minutes for small groups (six carbon copies) this would prove to be quite a challenge.

After progressing from typing syllabuses and the usual correspondence, I was then introduced to the study tour programme which Southern district was very involved with. This was a completely different area to work in – hotels, coach/ferry companies, airlines etc. Some years we would have a national and international programme of up to fifteen different locations....Since those early days, I have worked in two districts with five district secretaries and numerous office and field staff, many of whom have become lifelong friends. I have worked in four different office locations and seen many, many changes in technology such as the introduction of the computer, scanner, photocopier, fax machine and franking machine. The funding for the WEA has changed often and each time it brought new changes with office procedures, with the biggest being the Further Education Funding Council and the introduction of the WEA's computerised management information system .

Diane Le Marechal, Thames & Solent District, 2002

WEA districts were established as the WEA developed from being a small membership and branch organisation to a more coherent national voluntary organisation in the period from 1907. Districts emerged and boundaries developed in response to local activism and the scope of the universities providing teaching for the tutorial classes. The network expanded to consist of twenty-one districts and remained relatively stable from the 1920s until a period of organisational restructuring from the 1980s onwards. The branches, and affiliated organisations, elect representatives on to a District Council, which in turn elects a District Committee, responsible for the work of a district secretary. This is the senior employee of each district, running an office, of which, in the early days, he would have been the sole employee.

The district secretary post has changed over time. Initially it incorporated a mixture of financial and academic management, and liaison with the voluntary movement, partner organisations and local government, on a scale not dissimilar to the role of tutor organisers today. As district programmes grew the role of tutor organiser began to absorb more of the day-to-day work of setting up classes. National roles for district secretaries have increased significantly in the last few decades and the paraphernalia of modern management systems absorbs more of their time.

District secretaries have been overwhelmingly male. Mary Silyn Roberts, who became secretary in North Wales district on the death of her husband, the serving secretary, in 1930, was the first woman to hold the post. A few women held less established positions: Miss G.A.Hutton was assistant district secretary in London district from 1917-1937. We know little about her life but a telling testament to her, on her retirement, was that 'her sympathetic treatment of the problems of branch and class secretaries has been one of the binding links in the district' (*London Bulletin*, 1936/7). In North Staffordshire Lillian Downes, school teacher, WEA

tutor and later head mistress of a Girls' High School was honorary joint secretary with E.S.Cartwright from 1921-23 and others undertook the role temporarily, sometimes without pay, during the First and Second World Wars. From 1947 until 1967 the post was exclusively male. During the 1980s and '90s more women were appointed; a whole generation of officers from the sixties were retiring and the traditional routes into the work – Ruskin College or trade union work - had by then a less symbiotic relationship to the WEA. The WEA district secretary had been a post held in some esteem within the wider Labour movement. By the '80s the world of trade unions had been weakened and adult education had massively expanded. Women came into the post as its status declined. By the late '80s women held *nearly* half of all district secretary posts, yet numbers declined again from the mid-'90s. As the new century unfolds women are still in the minority as district secretaries.

As the work of districts grew, the need for support began, from the 1920s, to result in the appointment of either assistant district secretaries – higher status and usually male – or clerks and typists – lower status and usually female. Their work, largely invisible to the outside world, has been the cement that has held the framework of classes, branches, committees, organisers, tutors and district secretaries, together.

What has it been like for women working in the district office? In the early days a traditionally male world for women district secretaries to negotiate and for women secretaries, administrators and finance workers, traditionally female occupations within an organisation that has been slow to change: technologically and managerially. The WEA regularly recruited students and volunteers into its offices – this guaranteed an informed and enthusiastic staff and sometimes added interest to what might otherwise be a routine job. It appears to have failed to offer much in the way of progression or development for those women. Here are a few of the stories from the district office.

Mary Silyn Roberts 1877 - 1972

This account was written by Annie Williams, district secretary of North Wales WEA, in 2003. She has drawn on two essays in a WEA publication Silyn, no.1, June 1994 by R. Wallis Evans. Annie writes, 'The WEA in north Wales remained in Rhoslas, College Road, the Silyns' house, until 2001 when the house became much too small for the activities of the Association particularly after it had merged with Coleg Harlech, Wales' only adult education college... I have now developed a keen interest in Mary Silyn Roberts and hope to find the time over the next year or so to write up her history.'

It is of particular significance to us in Wales that Mary Silyn Roberts was the first woman in the WEA to be appointed district secretary. She became district secretary for the North Wales district in 1930.

Mary was born in Mold in north Wales but grew up in London. The man whom she was to marry became a minister at Lewisham Chapel and in 1905 they moved to north Wales when Robert Silyn Roberts took up a new ministry in Tanygrisiau near Festiniog. This was a quarrying area with a close knit community that valued education. During this time Mary and Robert Silyn visited Denmark and became involved in the Tarm High School movement and came to know Peter Manniche. During the First World War Mary was appointed organiser of the Women's Land Army for the whole of Wales. She had three children but somehow managed to juggle all these responsibilities.

Her husband Robert Silyn became the founder of the WEA in north Wales in 1925. Between 1925 and 1930 he had set up fourteen new branches and had played an important role in establishing Coleg Harlech as an adult residential college in 1927. In 1930 they bought a house called 'Rhoslas' in College Road in Bangor that later became the office of the WEA district.

Mary was also a peace campaigner and a member of the Women's International League for Peace and Freedom. On 27th May 1926, 2,000 people, mainly women, gathered in the village of Penygroes in Caernarfonshire to give their support to the North Wales Peacemakers' Pilgrimage. This event marked the beginning of a journey to Chester that would take five days. On 19th June the North Wales Pilgrims joined up with 10,000 other women in Hyde Park under the banner 'Law not War'.

The group in north Wales, the Peacemakers' Pilgrimage was organized by a small number of women who had first met in Bangor in April 1926. Mary became one of its honourable secretaries. The group later became a branch of the Women's International League for Peace and Freedom. The activities of the group are impressive and involved a great deal of travelling abroad for conferences and campaigning events.

In 1930 Robert Silyn Roberts died suddenly on his return from a visit to Russia. On the journey back, his ship ran into a cloud of mosquitoes just before it passed out of Kiel Canal and he was bitten on his face. Within twenty-four hours he fell into a fever and died some weeks later at the age of 56.

The North Wales Committee asked Mary to take up the role of district secretary and she did this with great success. Her organisational skills were exceptional and during the war when petrol was short she found innovative ways of ensuring that lecturers were able to get to classes. Mary was an exceptional person who managed to combine family work and political commitments throughout her life. Her achievements need to be recorded.

Mary Stringer 1913-2001

This account by Zoë Munby draws on information provided by Jean Bould, Potteries WEA branch; Derek Tatton, Wedgwood Memorial College; WEA News, Autumn 1974; Fifty Years A-Growing, The History of the North Staffordshire District of the WEA, C.Scrimgeour, 1973

Mary was born into a 'WEA family' – her father was Elijah Sambrook, a miner, blinded at work and yet active as a founder voluntary member and tutorial class student of the Potteries WEA. Mary attended her first tutorial class at sixteen years in Tunstall, Stoke on Trent. She because class secretary, then Tunstall branch secretary. She began working in the North Staffordshire district office in 1935.

In 1940 George Wigg, then district secretary in North Staffs., was given leave of absence to join the Army Education Corp. The district appointed Mary and Gladys Malbon as joint acting district secretaries in his place. Gladys was a recently appointed Oxford staff tutor and the work was split between the two women, with both carrying an organising responsibility, Mary, at twenty-six years, managing administration and Gladys managing academic affairs. They were key figures in the campaign to found a local university that culminated in the opening of Keele University in 1950. The partnership continued until Wigg resigned when he became MP for Dudley in the 1945 election. Gladys was formally appointed as district secretary but resigned herself in 1947, moving to Cornwall where, as Gladys Harris, she continued WEA teaching and voluntary involvement.

Mary worked as finance officer at the district office until 1973 – thirty-eight years of service with six different district secretaries. In a voluntary capacity she was active in planning and woarking on the annual garden party at Wedgwood Memorial College. She was a magistrate. She represented Tunstall as a Labour councillor for the City of Stoke on Trent from 1961-86 and was on Staffordshire County Council from 1973 to 1997, being especially active on Social Service and Education committees. In all her work she travelled by public transport: no small feat from Tunstall to Stafford as a County councillor at eighty-four years.

Bim Andrews

Bim Andrews and her daughter Sue Gardener

These are extracts from a much longer autobiography written by Bim in the 1980s. Her daughter, Sue Gardener, was a WEA tutor organiser, voluntary member and was active in the Women's Education Advisory Committee in the 1980s. Sue was interviewed for the WEA Women's History Project and passed on a copy of her mother's autobiography to the project.

In theory, I became responsible for myself, and, in a crunch, free to defy my parents. To reach this landmark, and to get a new job which paid me £2 a week, did lead to changes. I began work as what would now be called personal assistant to the secretary of the Eastern district Workers' Educational Association. I was half the office staff and he was the other half. We had a very smart office in a charming house, wholly occupied by the University Extra Mural people, mostly male and hard to handle, after the clerks and shop boys at the Co-op....

When I got the WEA job I had already been attending a literature class. My first – Dr Ratty, a Unitarian minister, on Bernard Shaw and Samuel Butler. More glory. I was in any case reading widely and indiscriminately. Most of it was managed in bed. I couldn't keep the gas jet burning, because the wood-panelled wall which divided me from the landing had cracks in it. So I bought candles, and read by a flickering light, shielded when anyone was about. Beverley Nichols, Florence Barclay, Marie Stopes, E. M. Forster, Leslie Weathered, Shelley's *Defense of Poetry*, Bennett and Wells, and lots of forgettable contemporary novels....

I cannot now enter into a mind which could encompass *Marriage and Morals*, containing aphorisms from Bernard Russell like 'the more civilised people become the less capable they seem of lifelong happiness with one partner', as well as my Sunday school class and my Brownie pack. 1930 was the year when changes began, but it took at least three years to slough off the old ideas, attitudes and modes of self-expression. Perhaps because they were the mesh into which my friendships fitted. Very warm friendships; male and female. Fellow Sunday school teachers most of them, in particular one large family....

I think that my life was frenetic. Reaching out to new experiences, all of them meeting a deep need in me, and yet confined by the existing commitments and unable to give them up. I felt more secure and in control with them than with the new people I met in WEA. These enfolded me later....

I often didn't get to Sunday school, and no wonder. It was the only morning when I could rest. My boss didn't work on Saturdays, but I did. Sometimes on Saturday afternoons too, if there was a District Council meeting. These I enjoyed tremendously, scribbling shorthand, serving teas, measuring myself up against Extra Mural students from mining areas or agricultural backgrounds, tutors and branch secretaries. The people went very much to my head, particularly the evidence which suggested they found me interesting. Heady is the word, and I made mistakes. About people, I mean....

My boss at the WEA was also opening doors for me. I went to Stratford-on-Avon with him and his wife, to look with a wary eye on this modern theatre – he joined the critics who thought it looked like a brewery. I tended to feel that if it was new it must be good....

It certainly was a heady time, with much on offer.... At our own summer school – Cheshunt in Cambridge – I mistook the atmosphere of affectionate attention which surrounded me for benevolence great enough to ignore my cavalier attitude to working hours. I didn't see that my WEA boss saw my carry-on as neglect of him. He was a tight-lipped chap who brooded. So when, against his advice I entered for and won a Cassel scholarship to London University he turned nasty. I hoped to work until the week before I had to set out for University College; I needed the money. The scholarship was worth £150. Not even the glory of my first bank account could hide the fact, when I had paid fees at UCL, I should be back with £2 a week to live on in London. After summer school was over at the end of July he gave me the sack – to save the WEA my salary in a slack season, he said. I should have appealed to the District Council, but we had no education in our rights as employees then. For two months I had to manage at home on a few shillings a week dole money.

I set off for London on my bike, to save railway fares, with my suitcase balanced on the handlebars and a parcel on the back carrier. 63 MILES, through Royston and Ware, and down the Great North Road. Well, Jude the Obscure walked into Oxford with his pack on his back. The fact that I was going to board with the parents of a chap I had met at summer school made this tough assignment possible. They were Salvation Army people, and how or why they endured my nonsense I shall never know. I suppose they enjoyed having their roomy house filled with WEA people, for it was here rather than at UCL that I found my real friends. I had chosen to study industrial psychology, for a postgraduate academic diploma, after three years work in an evening class held in the laboratory at Cambridge. I thought it touched the real world more closely than literature. Well, perhaps it did; but I am sure that it is my reading literature which has really informed me....

I was also up to my neck in all that London WEA had to offer, and allowing myself to be used by left-wing students like John Cornford and others who were active in the anti-war movement. Used, because I could do secretarial work; they were mostly middle-class and highly intelligent, strong on theory and impressed by my origins and practical skills...Along with all this politicking, I managed to see films, theatre, ballet and opera. My WEA friends effected these introductions for me. We were hooked on Rimsky-Korsakov's 'Snow Maiden', making regular visits to the gods at Sadler's Wells. We could sing most of it between us. Ballet stars Massine and Danilova at Covent Garden; Richardson, Geilgud and Olivier at the Old Vic for 9d, and all kinds of everything at the cinema. They introduced me to music too...

When I finished my year at university in 1934, with my postgraduate academic diploma in industrial psychology to launch me into a new job, the most important thing in my life was not my choice of career, but my participation in the activities of my friends. They centred round our camping weekends and many things flowed from this...I was working in a Juvenile Employment Bureau, still living with my Salvation Army friends. I was reluctantly involved in arranging for girls to come from the Distressed Areas in Wales and the north of England to take jobs as live-in domestics. Usually in households of modest means, and perhaps good intentions, though it was difficult to be sure of the latter. It might be a vicar's wife who badly needed help, or a bank manager's wife who needed social significance. It seemed right that the girls should be helped and wrong to help them in this way. One positive thing my mother had done for me was to keep me out of domestic service, and I was disturbed by the irony of my task.

At that time, in spite of my university experience, I didn't believe in my career any more than my juveniles did. We were 'riding into a gap', unless we had landed a job which carried a pension. If we were women, whose pensionable jobs had to be forfeited on marriage, how could we think of a career? As working class types, we didn't live in a society where people talked with mock modesty about their children's school successes, or measured their openings into wealth and status, as was the prevailing pattern when our children were going through the state educational system with its wider options. In the '30s we followed our noses in practice, and kept our ideas and enthusiasm for the prospect of social change. Sometimes WEA and Extra Mural opportunities brought theory and practice together and made for personal progress. A miner could, through Ruskin College, become a tutor in adult education or a Member of Parliament. For women, there were hints of the casting couch approach to this kind of achievement, and I daresay it was accepted by some women who refused to knuckle under. I also knew some who, unlike me, were admirably single-minded and resolute enough to get the jobs they wanted, and to break out of the strait jacket of a working class home by these means. They were the early heroines of Women's Lib. It was necessary to know what you wanted to do, and I certainly didn't. I wanted to do everything – I had big ideas about living and none at all about working.

Mary Harrold

Mary worked in the West Midlands district office from 1965 until her retirement, for the second time, in 2001. She wrote part of this account as an article in the Civil Service Council for Further Education Magazine *in the 1970s. She added to it for the WEA Women's History Project in 2001.*

When I was a teenager in the '40s I went to Local Education Authority classes for the usual vocational subjects, shorthand, typing and English. I did cause a minor disturbance during my last session because I dropped typing and took history. (Fancy anyone doing that voluntarily!) It seemed understood that you went to night classes for something useful – in no sense of the word could history be termed as useful.

For a number of years afterwards I decided that sitting in a classroom was not for me. After all, I had received a number of certificates and I thought that I could leave school behind me. I worked at a small ICI chemical works at Oldbury. My cousins had been members of the WEA for many years. I had heard them speak of the interesting lectures they had. This meant nothing to me because I thought of the agony of sitting in a classroom, probably only partially heated, listening to some dry as dust facts.

My own introduction to WEA activities was through coach trips, in 1962. I was induced to go on an evening run to a delightful manor house in Worcestershire. I found that the people who went on the trip were not earnest seekers of facts but friendly, ordinary human beings doing something which interested them.

They were members of a local history course taking advantage of the summer months to see some of the places and things about which the tutor had lectured during the winter. I found during the visit that I learned something about the house and the history of the period in which it was built but more than that I found that when I did venture an opinion it was listened to courteously. This made me feel that I must

go on the trips that followed because I enjoyed being with the group. Most people participated in some way and the tutor enjoyed himself hugely. I think it was this feeling of the enjoyment of learning that attracted me.

After this I decided that perhaps I had better try to find out more about the WEA. When I joined a WEA evening class the following autumn I came to realise the value of the freedom which resulted from the absence of the examination bogey. People went for the enjoyment of the subject not to cram to get a 'pass mark' at the end. I found that the students participated in the class by comments which created discussion or argument. Sometimes even a very shy person was goaded by some argument into a comment which led to a lively discussion.

I was bored with the ICI job, not with my work mates, who were super, so I wrote to the then district secretary about the possibilities of a job. I originally wrote asking if he knew if there were vacancies with a union office. I felt I wanted something of value to the community (rather pompous!). I didn't hear anything for some time, I had written it off when I had a letter saying there would be a vacancy in the WEA office fairly soon – so I waited and got the job. That was in 1965. I did correspondence and publicity, then gradually registrations for classes. Then minutes – I enjoyed meeting the people at meetings.

I went to WEA classes at Holt Road Primary School, Blackheath. We sat on primary school sized chairs! There was a branch at Blackheath at one time, small but lively. Now I go to a day-time class in Wolverhampton - this term on the American West since 1890. Most students prefer day-time; it's possible for West Midlands pensioners to get a pass for public transport between 9.30 am – 10.00 pm. This helps a great deal. It would be very expensive if I had to pay two bus fares each way. Most classes are extremely enjoyable, creating lively discussion.

Jean Barr

Jean was interviewed in 2002 for WEA Scotland's Centenary Celebrations. The account below consists of extracts from that interview, which are concerned with the experience of being a district secretary. Jean studied philosophy at Strathclyde University and taught sociology there in the '60s, in addition to some part-time women's studies teaching for the WEA. After the birth of her first child she travelled to Italy, where she taught English as a foreign language, before returning to Glasgow to work on an alternative newspaper, the Glasgow News. She later taught at Glasgow College of Technology and for the Open University, before her appointment in 1982 as district secretary for the West of Scotland district of the WEA, where she remained until 1991. Since that time she has worked in research, acquired a PhD and is currently head of department of Adult and Continuing Education at the University of Glasgow.

I was a kind of chief executive of the district. I suppose I saw myself as trying to engage people in a discussion about education and what it should be like - I was a very philosophical district secretary, because that's what I was interested in! Also how to do things in different sorts of ways, not just through committees or somebody standing in front of a classroom. I was interested in how the process involved in education was reflected in the organisation of the WEA. In terms of student involvement and being very empowering and enabling in the classroom and developing wonderful methods, it was good - it wasn't always wonderful at the level of its own organisation in involving everybody. That's true I think as a national organisation and at a district level. It's like any organisation because you're running as an organisation and trying to get things done....

I remember at the time thinking it's not really district secretary that I want to be, I'd rather be a tutor organiser because it's closer to the educational work, developing programmes and so on. In the end, I'm really glad that I was a district secretary because it gave you an insight to all sorts of levels of work, which were really interesting. The policy level was fascinating as well and that has been related to the writing work that I've done since....

I didn't take gladly to being the person who was in authority and tended to want to do things as a member of a team. Obviously that was a bit of bad faith on my part because in the end I had to make the decisions and advise the District Committee, although it was the District Committee that made the decisions in the end. It was a genuine voluntary organisation but I obviously had to get together the material and the arguments and so it was important how I felt about things. I tended to want to be a district secretary who involved the staff. I don't know to what extent it worked but that was my approach....

We had staff meetings and I regularly saw the staff but we certainly didn't have appraisal meetings or workload modelling. It was more laid back than that probably because there was a lot of contact with them. I would go out to the different divisions as well and see staff there. It wasn't very formal....

With the District Committee that was pretty formal. There was an internal management group, which was the secretary, chair, vice chair and treasurer, which met regularly, and then the District Committee. So there was an internal smaller group which met on a regular basis. They were pretty formal with minutes and briefing papers.... It was the job of the District Committee (to negotiate funding) but obviously I, as the chief executive, had to be the main person in the district who did that. The district chairman was very good - Jimmy Ingles and Alistair Nicholson were terrific chairs and they would be fully involved in that negotiation. When we had the major meetings with the Scottish Education Department (SED) or parliament (we used to go down to the House of Commons as well) there was always a voluntary member and usually the chairman or treasurer who would be there with me. They were fully involved in negotiations of that nature. I would do the one to one with the chief executive involved in community education in Strathclyde or with the SED but the political meetings would involve the voluntary movement fully....

As my role developed I became more involved in policy working groups at Scottish level and national level. I got involved in the Women's Education Advisory Committee (WEAC) and the Unemployment Working Group which was a national grouping. There was also a national working group in basic education, which I was centrally involved in as well.... When you're in the WEA for a while, it's a very seductive body. It pulls you in because it's such a network. You get to know people throughout the land and also internationally. It was a wonderful opportunity to get into international networks of adult educators and I learnt so much through that. It definitely broadens your canvas and opens up possibilities that you wouldn't have had if you'd stayed in a college or university. Particularly through the Women's Education Network and particular district secretaries whom I had allegiances with. It was through these connections, getting to know people, knowing who I wanted to work with and knowing that the best work comes out of people who have got connections and understand one another....

There was a bringing into the classroom ways of acting, ways of working which had belonged to that movement and when married to educational ideas could be really creative - like song, poetry, free association, the things that are just anathema in a class where the notion of rigour is about the best

argument. That kind of connection to different ways in which people express themselves created a really heady mix of methods where there wasn't one correct method and where together you could come up with new notions which weren't just a combination of different heads coming together. It was really creative I think and it couldn't have happened without a much more imaginative notion of how you create knowledge together, which is not just the power of the best argument. It's having a licence to discuss your experiences, develop, say, a group poem when you're doing politics; bringing different things together into a class as legitimate which can be quite challenging and threatening to people who have been used to having a very deductive educational experience.

Esther Morris

Ester Morris commemorated on a stamp as Miss Caribbean Free Trade Association, 1973

Esther, from London District, wrote this account for the WEA Women's History Project in 2003.

I was born in 1951 in the beautiful Caribbean island of Dominica, (not to be confused with our neighbouring island The Dominican Republic), the eldest of four children, to Stanley and Celia Fadelle.

In February 1973 I took part in the Commonwealth of Dominica's Carnival Queen contest and came second which entitled me to go forward for the regional crown of Miss CARIFTA (Caribbean Free Trade Association) in Grenada, where I won the crown - 2nd time for Dominica in three years. I was one of the two queens who featured on a Commonwealth of

Dominica postage stamp commemorating National Day 1973, replacing the queen!

I came to England in Autumn 1973 to take up a year's secretarial course at the Lucie Clayton Secretarial College in Kensington. I then worked at the Jamaican High Commission and the Grey Green Coach Company as a shorthand/typist before starting work at the WEA London district in October 1979, where I have been for the past 23 years. I started out as a clerical assistant and now work as an administrator for 30 of the 59 branches in the London district area.

I am married to Clynton, and we have four children, Giselle, Jehan, Vivian and Pia.

Carolyn Daines

Carolyn wrote this account for the WEA Women's History Project in 2003. She is one of seven female WEA district secretaries in our centenary year.

My first acquaintance with the WEA was in 1975, when having left my job as a teacher of English as a foreign language in Cambridge to await the arrival of my first child, I joined a history course put on by the St Ives WEA branch. I sat (uncomfortably!) on tiny chairs in a local primary school whilst learning something of interest, making new friends, and being inducted in the 'mysteries' of the WEA. Three months later I was elected secretary of the branch, a post which I held for ten years until I went back to full-time work in the Community Education Department of Cambridgeshire LEA.

Those of you with experience of the WEA will know that my quick rise from 'ordinary' student to branch officer has more to do with a shortage of people willing to do the job, rather than with my particular talents. My deep commitment to the WEA, however, springs from that period. The WEA offered me a way to keep my mind active as I adjusted to motherhood and an absence of professional status, a place to meet like-minded people, and a springboard into voluntary community work and eventually a new career in adult education.

In 1992 I came back into the WEA fold as district secretary of Eastern district, a job with an old-fashioned title, based in an 18th century building in the heart of Cambridge. (The appointment of a woman to the post – and an American to boot – probably caused a wave of alarm throughout East Anglia!) My worry that the job might become something of a backwater, with the WEA bypassed by the significant changes to post-16 education forecast for the 1990s, proved unfounded. The creation of the National Association and the inclusion of the WEA within the funding regime of the Further Education Funding Council, meant that management of change was a continuous focus of my job.

The district secretary is the senior manager of a district, in my case of a region of 7 counties, who has responsibility for all aspects of educational provision, staffing, finance, governance, and policy implementation. The work has changed a great deal in the ten years I have been with the WEA – which is the aspect I like most about the job. I have had the opportunity to help develop the national association, to change the culture of a rather inward-looking district, to increase the volume and range of our courses and students, and to improve the quality of our educational activities.

I was fortunate to take up post at a time when the WEA benefited from increased funding and a raising of its profile in the post-16 sector. This context enabled me to use my abilities and experience to develop the district, whilst at the same time requiring me to enhance my skills and knowledge as the management of adult and continuing education became more complex. I have benefited greatly from the excellent support of my district officers and committee members and from working with a strong staff team.

A typical week for me involves a 7am start and a 5pm finish – if I am in the office – with a file of reading to take home. Saturday work is quite frequent, as that is when many of the meetings involving voluntary members and tutor training events take place. The occasional Sunday morning is sometimes necessary to complete large tasks like budget and operational planning. One of the most important responsibilities I have is to see that my staff can carry out their jobs efficiently and effectively, so I spend a lot of time talking with them in person, on the phone, via e-mail, or in meetings. By keeping in touch with what they are doing I can ensure that the district systems are working in their interest and am therefore better placed to 'trouble shoot' when things don't go as planned. My weekly commitment also includes work for the national association both as part of the team of senior managers of the WEA and as an individual district secretary with tasks assigned to me by the general secretary.

Being a female manager in the WEA is relatively unproblematic, despite a disappointing lack of women at the highest levels of management. I think women managers in the WEA bring an open, supportive and focused approach to management which has helped to break down what I saw as an anti-management, 'boys-in the bar' culture when I first joined the WEA as a member of staff.

I know that I am very fortunate to have a job that is so varied, challenging and worthwhile. I feel that it is my responsibility to see that the staff that work with me think the same about theirs!

Women in the National Association

Memories of the scheming and piecing-out and persuading and arguing that built up the movement come flooding into one's mind. Everybody worked themselves to the last stretch and expected the same from their colleagues. Those who read this are getting adult education by an easier road but I cannot think they get the thrill that came to the early builders.

Alice Wall, first WEA national women's officer

In 1997 when Jake Bharier became President of the WEA and the style of the National Executive Committee (NEC) became more open, I found myself West Mercia rep on the NEC. Since then we have had another change of president, and thus of style of chairing the NEC, with a more formal 'gloss'. Now we are a national Association the governance and funding are more centralised. Since I started on the NEC the discussions have become more finance orientated, more technical, much more jargon-filled, and somehow have drifted away from the old education-centred model. Technology has imposed on us e-mails (which I still fail to capture)....I haven't quite managed to escape yet, though the much lamented Wendy Fenn did occasionally sit in for me during my absences abroad (if there wasn't a football match), but the end is in sight as, following mother's death I am now free to fulfil my 1962 ambition and move permanently to Switzerland some time next year.

Meiriona Bielawski, 2002

The story of women's contribution to the national WEA is complicated. There have been relatively few women involved at a national level, both within the voluntary management, and as employees. An assessment of what their impact is and has been would take more space than we have here. It could be argued that they have been both powerful and powerless, active and passive: the usual situation of people in a minority. The reasons for the shortage of women coming from the ranks of the district voluntary movement are hardly surprising: although active in branches and districts, constituting the majority on committees for many years, women voluntary members have been consistently less likely to hold office in the organisation. This means that they are unlikely to become district representatives on the National Executive Committee and even less likely to hold voluntary office nationally. The demands of participation on national committees are greater in terms of travel and time than a local role – always a difficulty for women who may have responsibilities as carers. It is significant that the women who have taken this step have been older (with no caring responsibilities), childless, or sufficiently affluent to be able to support an active voluntary career. Women are less likely to have opportunities to develop the skills and experience of committee work that would equip them for national office. This weakness in the voluntary governance of the organisation suggests that the organisation has not explored sufficiently ways in which to build a more representative national organisation.

Nationally the WEA has been governed by an Executive, and for much of its existence, a larger Council. The Council was, for several periods, exclusively male and at all other times, women constituted on average less than a quarter of all district representatives. The WEA deserves credit for the radical establishment of a national Women's Advisory Committee in 1907; less credit for disbanding it in 1915 and failing to re-establish another committee until 1979. The first Women's Advisory Committee had representation on the Executive and thereafter long periods of time passed when the senior voluntary management was all-male. In the post-war period the numbers of women began to creep up, but only in the last twenty years of its existence have significant numbers of women from the districts played a role in national management.

Those women who have achieved national voluntary positions in the Association were co-opted, invited and otherwise drawn in for their specialist expertise, mainly in adult education but also in the Co-operative movement and trade unions. The first Women's Advisory Committee was, inevitably, composed of women representing organisations and institutions outside the WEA. That pattern continued with women on specialist committees and the executive up until the 1980s. Women such as Shena Simon, Barbara Wootton, Mary Stocks and Mabel Tylecote may have had some short-term teaching experience with the WEA but they qualified for Executive and vice presidency because they were respected figures in the wider world of education. Their lives tell us more about the mechanism by which a tiny number of women achieve senior positions in the world of education, than they do about the WEA. The interesting exception to this pattern is Ellen McCullough, who had a career in the trade unions and became the WEA's only female president from 1967 to '71, and who resigned her post to work on a short-term project for the organisation.

The WEA has never had a woman general secretary or deputy general secretary. The first woman employed nationally, other than in a clerical capacity, was Alice Wall, the first women's officer, followed by Ida Hony, in the period up to 1915; they in turn were followed by four short-term war time appointments. From 1919, until Margery Marsh's appointment as national district organiser in 1954, no other women were appointed to a national officer post. From the '60s until the mid '90s there was, sporadically, a single women officer in the national office.

What is the significance of this for the kind of organisation that the WEA has been, and is now? We can suggest that it has been less exposed, than it might have been, to a whole range of ideas and developments. The structures and management practices of the WEA remain relatively untouched by the passing of time. Trade unions, the organisations in whose image the WEA was shaped, have reacted to challenge, re-made themselves in response to changes in society. The WEA less so. This may well be in part a symptom of a remarkably static body of voluntary members and employees. Yet the controlling influence of men, or the failure of women to make an impact on the national organisation, forms a significant part of the culture we find in the WEA today.

There is not the space to tell every woman's story here. Mary Stocks, suffragist, campaigner for family allowances and birth control, adult educationalist, was a great friend of the WEA – but her story has been told elsewhere. Other well-known women have been excluded for the same reason. The women selected here, in the short space we have available, are a pioneering group who have individually contributed significantly to the organisation, and whose stories are in danger of *not* being heard.

Alice Wall 1884-1974

This account by Zoë Munby is based on information provided by Alice's daughter, Ruth Dewey, supplemented by the minutes of the national WEA Women's Advisory Committee, reports in The Highway *and Mary Hughes, 'Rediscovering Women Adult Educators' in* Adults Learning, *Vol. 2, No.4, December 1990.*

Alice was born in Oswestry, the daughter of a tenant farmer who died when she was six. She owed her education to an aunt who, with no children of her own, recognised in Alice something different and planned and managed to pay for a boarding school education at Wellington School for Girls. From here Alice won a university scholarship and went to Aberystwyth University in 1902. She graduated with a 1st Class London External degree in English literature. At Aberystwyth she met her future husband, Thomas Huws Davies, another working class student who had managed to get to university against harsh odds. They were not to marry for some years. On graduation, Alice worked for a year in London as education officer for the YWCA, a post in which she was not entirely happy, owing to the fundamentalist ethos of the organisation. When her mother became ill, she returned to live with her and to teach for two years at a local Grammar School. Her appointment, in 1910, as women's officer for the WEA, was at the suggestion of Tom Jones, the first treasurer of the WEA in Wales, later Secretary to the Cabinet, and, amongst his many activities, founder of Coleg Harlech, the Welsh adult residential college. Tom had known Alice through contacts at Aberystwyth and believing that her talents were being wasted, had told Albert Mansbridge, the general secretary of the WEA, about her.

Alice's post was paid for from independent fund raising, organised by the Women's Advisory Committee. The National Executive had only agreed to the post on condition that it did not draw on mainstream WEA funds. She was immediately busy, travelling around the country, speaking to WEA branch and district meetings, encouraging the formation of women-only classes, women's sections and women's committees within branches. One national leaflet and a pamphlet survives from this period, *Women in the Workers' Educational Association*; although carrying Ida Hony's name on its cover as secretary of the Women's Department, it was probably written in 1912 by Alice. It makes the case for women-only education and explains how to form women's sections, describes types of classes and suggests how women's education may develop in the future. *The Highway* documents the impact of her work: in the period 1908 to 1910 there had been women-only classes in five towns and cities. In 1910/11 these spread to nine locations, seventeen in the following year, each often accounting for more than a single class. Birmingham, London and Bristol hosted enormous programmes of courses, lectures, study circles and events. The extraordinary expansion of WEA women-only education from 1910-1915 owes its impetuous to the tide of political activism in the suffrage movement. Its expression in the WEA – at this period effectively the educational arm of women's suffrage – would not have been possible without Alice's energetic organising and later that of Ida Hony.

Apart from Albert Mansbridge, Alice was for a period the only national WEA employee. She was theoretically only employed on a part-time basis but recalled that the demands of the national office meant that she was responsible, in reality, for anything which Mansbridge did not get around to doing. This involved catching aspiring 'golden youth' who visited the great man in the hope of joining the great work, and selling them a copy of *Oxford and Working Class Education* (the original report on tutorial classes) for 2/6 on their way out. She is officially recorded as secretary of the Evening Courses Committee by 1911. *The Highway*, the WEA journal, which came out nine months of the year, was a huge job in which Alice was heavily involved. She remembered Mansbridge as an exciting, but difficult personality to work with. She supplemented her organising income with teaching tutorial classes and recalled rushing off to the British Library from the office for last minute preparation squeezed in amongst the demands of her office work. A student of hers, a seamstress at John Lewises, made a christening gown for Alice's first child years later.

Alice left her post on marriage to Thomas Huws Davies in June 1912 and planned to continue teaching her tutorial classes. However, she suffered a miscarriage and a subsequent infection left her ill for a number of years. She had been worn down by the pace of work with the WEA and believed that it had left her vulnerable to ill health. Thomas took over her interrupted class and Alice did no further paid work until the Second World War, when she worked in welfare for the Ministry of Labour. However, throughout her life she remained busy and committed to a number of voluntary causes.

Thomas Huws Davies was a civil servant who had worked on the Welsh Church Bill, was Secretary of the Welsh Church Commissioners and involved in a number of Welsh political and cultural activities. Thomas and Alice were friends of Robert Silyn Roberts and his wife Mary, Welsh socialists and activists. Robert Silyn became the first district secretary of the WEA in North Wales and Mary took over from her husband on his death in 1930. Alice's connection with the Silyn Roberts's places her in the heart of Welsh adult educational activism. After the First World War the Ministry of Reconstruction established a committee to report on the future for education. Alice was one of only two women on this committee and wrote a section in what became known as *The 1919 Report* on 'Women and Adult Education' with Marion Phillips, who was co-opted onto the committee for this purpose. Alice also exerted pressure to ensure that sufficient references to Welsh issues were included in the report. She subsequently contributed an article on women and adult education to the 1920 *Cambridge Essays on Adult Education*. She was secretary to the Board of Governors of Coleg Harlech from its foundation in 1927 and remained involved with it for many years. Family holidays in Harlech combined a break from London with visits to the college. She established a seven-year covenanting scheme to support the college and her daughter recalls her house as full of the index cards used to record her work with the college. She remained in touch with the WEA also via a friendship with Ida Hony, who took over the post of women's officer that she vacated. The Huws Davieses would visit Ida's family in Oxfordshire, where their children would play together.

Alice's involvement with the Labour movement dated back to membership of the Independent Labour Party, in Oswestry, a branch that she described as consisting of herself and five railway men. She worked on the practical day-to-day business of politics, in the Women's Labour League and later in the Labour Party in London. She was also active in the League of Nations Union.

In the 1920s Alice had a son, James, and a daughter, Ruth. The family lived in Camberwell, then Kew, near London. Her husband Thomas died in 1940 and from 1951 she spent increasing amounts of time in America with Ruth, by then married. She moved there permanently when she was eighty.

WHAT WOMEN WANT TO KNOW.

WOMEN, just as much as men, want to know more about the world in which we live, and want to equip themselves better to serve their fellows.

But it often seems very difficult for a working woman to make use of "educational" opportunities. The housewife finds it impossible to leave her home in the evening, which is the time when the men folk go to their classes. The afternoon, therefore, is often the only time when she could be free for a class or lecture or meeting.

Again, women have not, as a rule, had the same experience of public work, or the same opportunities of common discussion as men ; their membership of trade union and labour organisations is comparatively new, and what social life there is in the factory ends for the majority of women at marriage.

Nobody wants to join a class where she will appear ill-prepared in comparison with the others. The result is that a woman is often shy of joining a mixed class where she thinks that many of the others will have more experience in speaking and writing than she has had ; and where some of the members may have read a good deal in the leisure time that the woman worker nearly always has to give to household duties.

HOW THE W.E.A. CAN HELP.

The W.E.A. exists to meet these difficulties. It will provide classes for men and women, classes for women only, classes in the afternoons as well as in the evenings. A group of women belonging to some society, perhaps a Co-operative Guild, who already know one another, can have a class specially arranged for *them* if they like.

The W.E.A. will provide **elementary classes**, where those who have had no opportunity of study since they left school can meet and talk over and read about the subjects that interest them, whatever these may be, *or* the W.E.A. **will arrange more advanced classes** for those who have had greater opportunities,

Ida Hony 1885-1977

This account by Zoë Munby is based on the minutes of the national WEA Women's Advisory Committee, and reports in The Highway; *Ida's obituary in the* Wiltshire Gazette, *October 1977 and the introduction to re-prints of her books.*

Ida was born the second of six children of the Reverend Charles Hony, of Bishops Cannings in Wiltshire, and his wife Annie. Annie was not a typical parson's wife: she wrote, entered literary competitions, and showed little interest in domestic affairs. She allowed her children to run barefoot and put the girls in practical serge drawers. Ida herself wrote from childhood. As an adolescent she had studied at Oxford although it is unclear if she was formally attached to one of the women's colleges. Influenced by the ideas of Temple and Gore she returned to Wiltshire and established a WEA branch at Woodborough, against local opposition. They 'thought education for village people was a back door to socialism'; however, Ida was helped by Reuben George, the founder of Swindon WEA branch, and her father. The branch flourished. In May 1912 the branch performed a play that Ida had written. When Alice Wall left her post as national WEA women's officer in June 1912, Ida replaced her, aged 27 years. Her younger sister Sibyl was teaching a women's literature class in Bristol in the following year, extending the family connection with the WEA.

Ida picked up on the wave of expanding women's classes and, following in Alice's footsteps, travelled the country to promote separate women's structures within the WEA. The booklet *Women in the Workers' Educational Association* identifies Ida as running the WEA Women's Department and she may have helped complete its publication. She certainly continued to write, publishing a poem and articles in *The Highway*. She led a discussion at the women's meeting during the 1913 WEA annual conference. By 1913/14 there were 33 women's branches and committees. Ida's travels were often related to the formation of new WEA branches and she is sometimes reported as holding separate women's meetings.

Ida's post in the Women's Department was a temporary contract, extended on two occasions, until March 1915, when she was appointed to another temporary post, now part-time, with responsibility for developing classes in rural areas. She was moved at Easter to a base at the WEA's residential centre, Buxton Cottage at Kingswood Common near Henley. Here, is was announced, she 'would conduct specific experiments', this was probably an attempt to work with rural organisations, in the way that the WEA had established partnerships with the trade unions and co-operative societies. Ida appears to have remained secretary to the women's committee in a voluntary capacity. In the last report of this committee, in November 1915, Ida's marriage and resignation are recorded. Subsequently the national association announced the dismantling of the Women's Advisory Committee, ostensibly because there were now active local committees, as well as a very strong London WEA Women's Committee.

At some point in the course of her WEA work Ida met Thomas Gandy, an Oxfordshire GP who shared her concerns for social justice. They married in 1915 and lived for the next fifteen years at Peppard, in Oxfordshire. Ida was an adventurous woman, relishing an offer in 1912 of a flight in an open bi-plane over Salisbury Plain with the Royal Flying Corps, 'all flight has seemed tame after that'. Later, in the 1920s, she would take her children on relaxed camping trips which would have scandalised more conventional GP's wives. 'Starting off with her children at sunrise with a small tent, a sleeping sack and a basket of food with no firm idea of where they would spend succeeding nights except that a south west corner of Shropshire on the corner of Wales looked a tempting rich brown on the map.'

In the years that followed Ida described herself as a 'quarter time author'. She combined bringing up her three children with a steady flow of writing. Following in her mother's footsteps she wrote and staged plays for local amateurs; she wrote children's books, reminiscences of her own childhood, stories of her eccentric aunts, local history – she published her last book in her ninetieth year. In 1930 Ida and Thomas moved to Shropshire from where she broadcast for the BBC on Shropshire life. She was involved in the Women's Institutes and was active in the Second World War in helping evacuees. When Thomas retired in 1945 they moved to Dorset but on his death, in 1948, she returned to Wiltshire and her last books were concerned with the county of her birth. She left an unfinished book of reminiscences that included an account of her WEA experiences.

Margaret James 1901-1943

Margaret's original bequest of £9000 accumulated into the Margaret James Fund, which largely financed the 1990s expansion of women's education in the WEA. This account of researching her life was written by Annie Winner, WEA tutor organiser in Thames & Solent district, in 2002-3.

In the early 90s, the Women's Education Committee of the WEA was charged with making the best possible use of the Margaret James Fund, which by then had accumulated to around £90,000, to support and develop women's education. One of the uses to which the money was put was the presentation of an award for best practice in women's education at each WEA biennial conference. Three of us committee members were discussing 'the speech' for the first award in 1997, and realised that we knew absolutely nothing about Margaret, apart from a rumour that her origins were in north Wales, and that she had died some time in the 1940s. While this enabled us to make a useful point about how women's history is often so veiled and unrecorded, the fact that Margaret remained a mystery was frustrating.

So, when in 2001 a project was begun to research and archive the contribution made by women to the development of the WEA to mark its centenary, it seemed the right moment to try to find out more about Margaret James.

As a totally novice amateur sleuth, where could I start? All I had was the North Wales rumour – which turned out to be unfounded - and another suggestion that she might have been connected to East Midlands district. I started with the WEA archives in the University of North London, searching through the East Midlands district *Annual Reports* for the 1930s and '40s. This turned up a reference to a Miss Margaret James MA, PhD, who had been an individual subscriber from 1937-1943 (contributing between 5/- and 10/- annually). This designation implied that she was not married (so at least James was probably the right name to look for); that she was likely to be an Oxford or Cambridge graduate; and that her doctorate was from some other university.

In the national WEA *Annual Reports* of the time, I found that her bequest of over £9000 is first mentioned in the WEA's *Annual Report* for 1947/48. It appeared again in 1948/49, when the WEA is described as 'negotiating with universities and the Ministry of Education as to the best use to which this bequest can be applied.' In The Highway for January and April 1949 applications were invited for Margaret James University Scholarships for Women.

> 'The scholarship will be awarded by, and tenable at, the University of Manchester commencing in the October term 1949. Applicants must be women to whom entry to a university at a normal age was impossible because of financial circumstances, and who have followed appropriate courses of study preferably in classes arranged by or in co-operation with the WEA. (From the April edition)'

In *The Highway* for July/August 1949 the first award was announced. The first scholar was 'Miss Edith F. May of the Romiley WEA Branch. Miss May is a Civil Servant and convinced the awarding committee, on which I was pleased to serve, that she was a student of outstanding ability'. The Fund is also mentioned in the financial reports of the time and by 1954 was valued at £12,130 11s 5d.

Girton College, Cambridge came up with a Margaret James who was born in 1901, in Nottingham, but as our Margaret presumably had a normal life span and had died in the 40s, this was unlikely to have been her. Nottingham High School for Girls found a Margaret James, born in 1892 – but her other biographical details didn't fit; the University of Nottingham had details of the Margaret James Scholarship but nothing else; the Nottinghamshire Archives Office had some information about a Margaret James, including, significantly, the name of a book she had published in 1930.

In the meantime I had sent off to the Probate Registry for a copy of her will. This arrived six weeks later, together with a copy of the Grant of Probate to her estate. Her will, made in 1935, was brief. She left half her possessions to her three brothers, Clement, Alfred and Arthur James. The other half she left to

> 'The President of the Workers' Educational Association, Professor R.H. Tawney, 441 Mecklenburg Square, London WC1 to be used by him for the founding of a University Scholarship for the benefit of a working class woman, preferably a member of a Workers' Educational Association class. The exact terms of the bequest are to be decided by him.'

The Grant also stated the exact date of her death, and revealed the full names, occupations (master draper and chartered accountant) and addresses (Edwalton on the outskirts of Nottingham, and the City of London) of her two surviving brothers.

Armed with the date of her death, I was able to find out where she died (Nottingham) and her age at death (42) from the General Register Office Index. This led me to her exact date of birth (March 2 1901 – so she was the Girton girl after all). I was then able to obtain her death certificate – which gave her cause of death: 'Suicide by throwing herself from an upper window whilst the balance of her mind was disturbed'. Her occupation is described as 'Spinster – lecturer in economics', and the place of death as 5 Arboretum Street. I tried to get the records of the inquest, but these were probably destroyed during World War Two. I was also able to get her birth certificate, which describes her father as a master draper, and shows that she was born at 15 Arboretum Street, Nottingham.

Back I went to the archivist at Girton, who came up with a lot more information, now that we knew we were on to the right Margaret. She found that Margaret had indeed attended Nottingham Girls' High School, and Girton College, Cambridge as a College Scholar to read history. From there she gained two research studentships to study for her PhD from the University of London. The Girton records also detailed her career. From 1927-1931 Margaret worked as assistant lecturer in history at the Royal Holloway College, during which time she had a couple of books published (*The City Livery Companies*, 1928 and *Social Problems and Policy in the Puritan Revolution*, 1930). From 1935 she worked part-time in the Department of Adult Education, University of Leicester.

Although I'd found out plenty during this extremely unlinear process, there were still many really important questions which had not been answered. What were her links with the WEA? I was intrigued by the fact that she'd left the money for the WEA to RH Tawney in person, which led me to try to find out more than I already knew about him. He was, of course, not only the vice president and president of the WEA from 1920-1945, but simultaneously worked at LSE, becoming professor of economic history from 1920-1949. So could Margaret have done her PhD at LSE? The answer – when I contacted the archivist there - turned out to be yes. She gained her PhD in 1927 and was also the winner of the Hutchinson Silver Medal in 1926. LSE records also show that she published articles in *The Times*, City of London Number in November 1927, and the *American Encyclopaedia of Social Sciences* in 1932. Finally, in her 1930 book, at the end of the Introduction Margaret wrote:

'To Mr RH Tawney, under whose direction I worked for three years, I owe a debt which it is impossible to express.'

The desire to find out more about Margaret, and ideally to obtain a photograph of her – led back to the possibility that her brothers might have had children who might still be alive. I wrote off to the 2 addresses in Arboretum Street in Nottingham where she had been born and died. This brought a phone call from the head's secretary of Nottingham Girls' High School which coincidentally now occupies these houses. She, together with the school's archivist, produced more information about Margaret 's schooldays, and her family. Further research found an account in the school Newsheet of 1942-43 of her 'sudden' death in 1943, which added the information that

'on her return to Nottingham she occupied herself with lecturing for the Workers' Educational Association, and in writing….She was also a very active member of the Anglo Russian society.'

What was the story behind her tragic end? Suicide rates are nearly always reduced in wartime, suicide was still a crime in 1943 – would putting 'while the balance of her mind was disturbed' on the death certificate be a way of dulling the stigma? Was she really mentally ill in some way, or had some other personal tragedy precipitated such a violent and painful end.

How did she get to be so academically distinguished? It was rare for a woman of her time from any background, let alone hers, to go to Cambridge and subsequently take a doctorate – how did this come about, and was she encouraged in her ambitions by her family or not?

Another big question is – where did she get all that money? Her estate was worth a total of over £19,000 – a considerable sum in the 1940s. She hadn't married it, could hardly have made it from her profession, and it seems unlikely that she could have made it herself – presumably she had inherited it from her family.

So, although I managed to find out quite a bit about the facts of her life, as a person she remains a bit of a mystery. We can only assume from the available information (including a mention as an associate in the 2003 obituary of the Oxford Marxist historian Christopher Hill) that she was a bright and academically gifted woman. She was one of numerous siblings from a well-to-do family. She presumably became involved with the WEA through her relationship with RH Tawney – which maybe developed her interest in working class women's education – and she came to a tragic end. It seems a particularly sad irony that a woman who was, for whatever reason, driven to suicide, never knew the immense benefit to probably thousands of women that her generosity provided. Not only were there the early recipients of the university scholarships, but since the early 1990s the Fund has been used to support dozens of development projects in women's education; to develop new programmes for women; for the Margaret James award for good practice in women's education, and in many other ways.

Sources

WEA Archive at the University of North London
Probate Registry
HM Coroner for Nottinghamshire
General Register Office Index
Nottingham Evening Post

Nottingham High School for Girls (special thanks to Christine Huett and Nancy Hudson)
Nottingham Registration District
Girton College Cambridge
University of London, Institute of Education

University of London, London School of Economics
University of London, Royal Holloway College
University of Leicester
The Highway

Elizabeth Monkhouse

Elizabeth was interviewed in 2002 for WEA Scotland's Centenary Celebrations from which the extract here is taken. She was born in Cheshire and studied French at Somerville College, Oxford. On graduation she taught English at the University of Poitiers whilst working for her Doctorate. This was followed by teaching French at a school in St.Andrews. During those years she helped revive the Labour Party branch and from this involvement became interested in adult education. She secured an introduction to Frank Jacques, district secretary of the Eastern district and began working in Norfolk as a tutor. In the summer of 1942 she worked in south west Scotland organising classes in industrial camps, which is described below. From there she worked as an organising tutor in Aberdeen, taught for the WEA in Manchester and then worked as a tutor organiser for the Extra Mural Department of London University from 1947. She was elected on to the WEA National Executive Committee in 1951 and became deputy president of the WEA in 1971 until 1993.

I was asked if I would like to have a go at a project in south west Scotland, where there were a lot of industrial camps at the time. People were building factories, airfields, putting up buildings for the RAF, mending aircraft, all sorts of things. The men there were living in dreadful conditions and they were very unhappy and very difficult. The employers had asked various voluntary organisations what they could do to help. The Ministry of Labour and the WEA together agreed that they would raise the money to pay for somebody for three or four months to provide what they called 'informal educational activities' - and boy, were they informal! The WEA put me forward and the Ministry of Labour man tried to persuade me that a fate worse than death was lurking behind every bush and I would do far better going to work in the Ministry of Labour. But that really wasn't on my agenda so I went to Scotland.

It started in May 1942 and went on until the autumn and then there was no more money. I had to go round to all the camps and talk to the agents and get their permission. I had letters of introduction from the Ministry of Labour but got very different receptions. Some of them said, 'Alright, we will have a try if you like,' one said, 'I'd thank you not to waste my time.' But on the whole, in the end, they agreed to let me have a go. And it was very difficult first of all. How do you get in touch with several hundred men working on an industrial site? The sites they were working were runways in the making or buildings in the making but the men themselves were lodged in huts as dormitories, with one extra for so-called recreation and one extra for the canteen, that's all they had. The washing facilities were a few standpipes, and I suppose enamel basins. Food was plentiful but very crude. I remember eating in the canteen with them and they didn't have mugs, they had slop basins and I asked the canteen manager why and he said, 'Well, they would abuse the handles if they had mugs.' I wasn't quite sure how you would abuse the handle of a mug. The only sort of entertainment they had, other than work, was a catholic priest who would come round once a week to say mass. They would go into Stranraer and get drunk and then one evening they would play pitch and toss, but that was all there was, except me appearing once a week, which was quite a change.

These were men of working age, in their 20s and up to about 50 or 60. A great many came from Ireland; a good many from Scotland of course, but not many from England. One of the difficulties was that first of all I had to find out what they were interested in. Most of them were interested in the war, why we were in the war, what our allies were like, what our enemies were like, and that I taught myself, which was fairly easy. But as to the others, some of them were very difficult to get going at all. In one of the camps, the first night, I got none at all. I had stuck up hand made notices on all the trees but nobody came at all and somebody explained to me that the paper notices were too big so they wrapped their laundry in them and that's why nobody appeared.

That lot were very difficult to get moving. However, I sat with them in the canteen eating and listened to what they were talking about, and to my surprise they were talking almost exclusively about income tax. They had never been in the income tax bracket before and these awful notices kept appearing and they tore them up and hoped that they would go away. Of course, more notices came, this time with red on them, so they really became worried about it. I nudged one of them and said, 'Would you like me to get hold of somebody who knows about taxation?' And he said, 'Would you?' They were terribly pleased about this and somebody came up and said, 'It's the first time anybody has ever asked us what we want,' which really told its own tale. I did find a wonderful tax official in Stranraer and he could ride a bicycle, and had one, so we got him out to the camp. He explained to them the difference between indirect and direct taxation and why direct taxation was so much fairer. So that although they didn't like paying income tax, on the whole it was better for them. And he got to know them quite well and it became a short course on economics.

It was difficult to get people to come. I did manage to get the rector of the Academy at Stranraer, he had a small projector and I got some films about Russia, which they very much wanted to see, and he agreed to bring it along. He said, 'I will bring it myself, I will only allow myself to work it.' So one Sunday evening, just as all the good folk were going to the church, the rector of the Academy was seen on the back of an open lorry, with an unknown young woman, driving off to the industrial camps for an evening of film....

At McAlpine's camp, where they were building for ICI, I had been there for a few weeks and the men started asking me about health. So I persuaded the County health officer to come and talk to them, and of course he had transport too. He talked to them a bit about health in a general way, and one of them started nudging the others and said, 'Are rats dangerous?' And he said, 'Yes, very dangerous, have you got them here?' They roared with laughter and said the place was crawling with them so he made a quick note. Later on they said, 'How long is a man to do heavy manual work without a little something to eat or drink?' and he said, 'Not more than four hours, at the outside,' and they fell about laughing again.

The next week when I got there I heard the agent's voice saying angrily, 'Has that bloody interfering bitch arrived yet?' So something had been going on behind my back. It turned out that the sanitary inspector had turned up at the camp to look at the rats under the building and had given McAlpines a bit of a hiding. Then what they described as 'Miss Monkhouse's man' had sent someone along to explain that they ought to have cups of tea more frequently. As the agent explained to me, 'If only they had waited, we were about to arrange something for them. You see, they used to build little fires all over the site and have little cans boiling up on them which was a terrible waste of time, it really was.' They had arranged to get a trolley that would go round with the tea, but the men had come up and said that Miss Monkhouse's man had said that they ought to have things more frequently and they weren't going to stand for it. He said, 'If only they had been sensible, we would have let them have these things.' I said, 'Did you tell them that?' And he said, 'No, we told them that we would give them their cards.' Which of course, in wartime, they couldn't, it was illegal, but the men were not too sure about it. I said, 'I'm sure if they knew, we could get them to agree to the arrangement.' 'Alright, you go and do it.' I had to go down and face the chaps and say, 'Look, they have made absolute fools of themselves but you've made pretty good fools of yourselves too.' So it was not only teaching for the WEA but a bit of industrial relations going on too, which was rather fun.

Eileen Aird

Eileen wrote That Was in Another Country *for the WEA Women's History Project in 2003.*

I worked in women's education from 1974 to 1995, initially for the Department of Adult Education at Newcastle University, then for the WEA Northern district where I was an organising tutor in women's education and after that for the national office of the WEA as an assistant general secretary with responsibility for women's education, tutor and voluntary member training and curriculum development. Finally I left the WEA to become principal of Hillcroft College for Women. Currently I am the director of the Women's Therapy Centre in London.

This is a progression from education to psychotherapy which made absolute sense for me: my interest in women's education was always in the wider identity change which took place not just in more narrowly focussed educational development.

The ten years from 1975 to about 1986 was a heady time to work in radical adult education. Resources, which seemed limited at the time but now seem abundant, were available without too many strings attached to develop exciting and innovative curricula. There were many colleagues willing to develop and teach on courses and for several of them this was part of their commitment to second wave feminism. The work flowed out into debates, conferences, late night meetings around supper tables, lunches with children alongside. There were conflicts and struggles as well as sisterhood and excitement. Nevertheless I remember this period as the richest time of my working life, shot through with an idealisation which no longer seems possible but also based in hard shared work to establish courses, draw in women who would not usually come to WEA classes, set up child care and crèches, campaign both within and without the WEA for women only provision.

Angela Martin's cartoons have been used to illustrate WEA women's education and in particular women's health training materials since the 1980s.

Chris Scarlett

Chris has been national co-ordinator for women's education with the WEA since 2001. Before that she worked as a tutor organiser in the East Midland district. She wrote the account, from which this extract is taken, in 2003.

My first contact with the WEA came in 1971 in Nottingham when I joined a memorable course with Bill Silburn and Ken Coates. I'd read their book on poverty in St Annes, Nottingham, and got inspired to join their research project which they set up with the WEA class members doing the foot slogging. I remember being told about the WEA in this class and being swiftly bullied into being class secretary. I was a bit taken aback at the time. Didn't tutors do that stuff? I had to in my day job. But I slowly caught on to the WEA philosophy and came to the conclusion that the WEA was both quite wonderful and completely potty - a view that hasn't noticeably altered over the following three decades....

A few years later on I joined a WEA class again as a student. This time in Wakefield, it was a course of its time, entitled 'Women's Studies'. I can't imagine any other organisation which would have a run a course like that one. It was electrifying. We talked and argued until we were exhausted. We begged to have another term, then another, then just another. The tutor found us speakers and materials which blew open our minds, confronted our prejudices and challenged our complacency. Our ages ranged over seven decades and the younger ones were astonished out of our arrogance hearing the older women talking about their fights for union recognition, their back street abortions, their war years as land girls. I'm sure that the Wakefield group was typical of many other WEA women's studies groups at the time. We stayed together as a women's group after the course finished...

Fast forward a few more years and I was back in Sheffield, a single parent and holding together an exhausting rag bag of six separate part time teaching jobs ranging from teaching in a maximum security prison to doing development work for women on a run down estate in Sheffield. It also included my first tutoring work for the WEA - a course grandiloquently entitled 'Citizens' Rights' in Clay Cross, Derbyshire,

for the Co-operative Women's Guild. Described, with a careful vagueness by the tutor organiser, as an interesting group of women who 'had their own way of doing things', I got my first experience of that particular bit of the WEA that has survived against the odds over the century. With the benefit of passing years which have thrown a softening glow over it, it was hilarious. The course was held - of course - in the room above the Co-op. A large empty space, with echoing bare floorboards, obligatory 40 watt bulb, and a raised platform at the far end, on which perched a piano, a table and several chairs, with two rows of seats lined up in front of it. A growing realisation led to the horrifying conclusion that as the 'guest speaker' I was up on the platform with madam president - an extremely able, confident woman who I never saw without her hat. The meeting - I realised, with mute despair, that it was indeed just that and couldn't by any stretch of the imagination be thought of as a class - started with minutes, matters arising, etc. I was startled to hear the next comment. At this point in the meeting they usually had a song before settling down to listen to the speaker. How did I feel about this? How I felt was pole axed with terror. I'd come prepared for the usual 'let's sit round a table and I'll lead this discussion' class. How on earth was I going to turn this into a 'talk'? Sure, let's have a song. *The Co-operative Women's Guild Song Book* was duly distributed and the piano - its significance now becoming crystal clear - struck up. At once I was taken back to my childhood chapel going days, recognising a familiar old hymn tune. The words were almost the same too- the Co-operative Spirit instead of the Holy Spirit. I gratefully opened up my lungs and sang. At the end of the song madam president gave me a discerning look, said I seemed to have enjoyed that one, so how about another. Great. If I really started belting it out we might be able to stretch this bit out. I did and they did. Eventually I had to give my 'talk' but that set the pattern for the next nine weeks. I was uneasily aware that I was learning more Co-op songs than they were learning citizen rights. Was I really earning my pay? No matter. We had found a way that seemed to work for all of us. It gave a whole new meaning to the notion of student - centred curriculum. Ten weeks up, madam president gave me a book token and told of her phone conversation with the tutor organiser who had rung up to see how it had gone. Splendid, she'd said. Christine is the best tutor the WEA has ever sent us. Good - oh. I'd done a bit better than I thought with citizen rights. Wrong. 'I told him,' she said, 'we can't say we were impressed with her views on citizens' rights, she's young and she's got a lot to learn. But by heck, that lass can carry a tune.'

Shaken by this experience it was a while before I chanced my arm with the WEA again. Come 1990 however, I found work as a tutor organiser for mid Derbyshire. It was a huge culture shock for me and for the first twelve months I wobbled badly. I'd come from working as an LEA adult education centre head, developing a women's 'Access to Higher Education' programme, community arts, DIY for women who renovated the centre café as their project. In Derbyshire I inherited a traditional branch programme with what I viewed as an unhealthy obsession with lead mining. But the second year in I began to come to terms with (and value) the traditional branch work whilst seeing possibilities for opening up the job. I started to develop links with local LEA community education workers and we jointly developed some outreach work. I gradually built up some women's courses, often with the solid support of the local branches plus a bit of opposition. Some of this work resulted, for a few years, in the Mid Derbyshire women's branch, which grew out of a 'Make Your Experience Count' course.

However, whilst this work was going on in the district, I had inadvertently got involved with the national WEA scene. I went on a WEA weekend conference for women's education held at Barlaston in 1991. Without realising it I had joined the WEA at a crisis point for women's education. Eileen Aird, one of the national officers, had recently left for another post and crucially for women's education, her vacated post wasn't filled.

The story of what happened next is a classic tale of women's relative power and positioning inside an organisation grown largely by women but dominated by men. The focus on women's education at national level was saved by a national office female administrator and researcher who managed to safeguard the budget earmarked for the women's education conference. The first evening session spelled out the position, and the weekend passed in a round of crisis discussions and plans. An ad hoc group of us agreed to meet up. We had no formal role or recognition within the national association but we intended to keep on meeting and planning anyway. Our strategy was to get a resolution passed at the 1993 biennial conference to establish a Women's Education Committee (WEC). We put in a lot of leg work and Swindon Women's branch put up the resolution. It got through. We'd got our committee and moreover we had money, via the Margaret James Fund.

With secretarial support from myself (half a day per week) we knew that we were no substitute for a full time female national officer promoting women's education. The first couple of years were intense as we slowly worked out the priorities but eventually we took the initiative. We would spend the Fund. It would be used to both support women's education work in the districts and to build support for women's education at national level. When it was spent we intended to have established an irrefutable case for funding women's education from the mainstream national budget. This process was helped by my national role becoming half time (paid for out of the Margaret James Fund). Over the following six years WEC found its confidence as a committee. A major national 'Women's Learning Programme' was developed. We set up a development fund to support women's outreach and development work in the districts. We continued the annual residential event. Lots more happened, but it's recorded elsewhere.

So in our Centenary year we still have a Women's Education Committee, we have four national women's education programmes, and a diversity and breadth of women's courses and projects in the districts. We have a national award for good practice in women's education. Women's education is more successful than the rest in reaching out to the most disempowered adults in our communities – which in part explains why the WEA still does lots of it. It needs it. Women's education now has mainstream funding from the national office budget, and we have finally achieved a full time post in women's education again.

So, a successful story of women's education at national level since Eileen's day? Well yes...and no. I am well aware that we have only got women's education on a liberal compromise in the WEA but – a big but – it's about the only place left in education which still gives some commitment to it. In so doing it attracts and keeps some exceptional women, who have made my working and personal life immeasurably the richer for knowing. It is a tribute to the WEA that I am happy to acknowledge.

Marian Young

Marion wrote The Vice-President's tale, my time in the WEA *in September 2002.*

This account begins at the end of a very active, working life which consisted of almost 30 years in education, part then full-time, working my way up, in schools and colleges, until I was holding down a very responsible, time-consuming and increasingly exhausting job. Because of financial problems in Newcastle upon Tyne, the city where I worked, the education service reduced drastically (by early retirement in my time) its school and college senior staff, the most expensive city staff members, and subsequently staff over 50 at other levels. Thus, heads, deputy heads, senior staff, senior college staff etc. - found themselves able to aspire to early retirement some years before they had thought this would be possible. A large number, including myself, did so, from almost every secondary school and college. What this did to provision in the city, it is not appropriate for me to discuss. In some cases, no doubt, it was a blessing. My husband had retired on health grounds almost two years before this. Suddenly, there we were, in our early 50s, able to start a new life. Wonderful !! We decided to move out into our beloved Northumberland countryside. We moved to a farmhouse in the depths of the country (stone, built 1870, in the vernacular style), and discreetly modernised, but not too much. I was terrified, excited and felt about 15.

So we moved. It was September and the countryside was so beautiful. The silence was unbelievable. The house was isolated, surrounded by wonderful views and about three quarters of a mile only from Bellingham our village. There are numerous scattered farmsteads, etc. in our neighbourhood, North Tynedale. We made many friends. For part of the first year, I was doing some work for Newcastle Education Service, helping to write and develop a study skills scheme for the city schools and helping to start an active learning team. This took up two or three days per week for 6 months or so. Then I was finally free.

On the morning of my second day of freedom, my nearest neighbour (a quarter of a mile up the hill from us) called and told me that I would have to come with her to an English literature class in the village that evening, as it would fold if they did not get some more takers. I protested. I had been teaching literature for most of my career, at first full-time, and then to cover the always uncoverable timetable when I held posts in secondary school management. My neighbour ignored my protests. It was a WEA class she said, as if this was sufficient explanation. 'A what?' I queried. Later that day, I found myself in a draughty school, thoroughly enjoying an argument about E.M. Forster with the unfortunate part-time tutor – later a great friend. The local tutor organiser turned up. It so happened I had worked with his wife some years earlier. He wondered if we could use my house for a meeting of locals who might be interested in setting up a branch. Bellingham needed its own branch, he said. Some days later our sitting room was filled with strangers. While I was out making tea for all, I was elected secretary of what became Bellingham branch, probably the smallest and most troublesome branch in the Association. I think this only when I am trying to organise the programme. I am chair again this year. I am always chair, or vice-chair, or secretary etc. although I would be really happy for others to take over the committee roles. Perhaps next year?

It just went on from there. My progress at district level was less to do with my abilities and more to do with a severe shortage of voluntary members who were prepared to become members of various committees (see previous paragraph). Unfortunately, this situation still pertains in several districts and branches. At a party in the tutor-organiser's home, the then district secretary (a poet, as was the above-mentioned tutor organiser) trapped me by flattery well beyond the call of duty. This flattery was ably supported by members of what was, I later discovered, the District Committee. I lapped it up and found myself on the District Committee. I still knew next to nothing about the WEA. I didn't know who were staff and who voluntary members, how long it had existed, what its aims were and how it was organised. I just didn't know how it worked. Nobody thought to tell me, but by the following year, when I became district chair, I had learnt a lot. (NB what the Voluntary Member Training Initiative tries to do some years later, is to answer these questions for other new voluntary members). Anyway, my feet have not touched the ground since.

After a couple of interesting years combining being district chair with National Executive Committee (NEC) representative for my district, I was asked to stand as a national officer – vice-president. I was elected and entered a new world. I became, and have remained since, chair of the Education Committee, a member of the officers' group, and a member of the Policy and Resources Committee. I am now a member of the strategic review group.

I have particularly enjoyed my work with the Education Committee. The committee's personnel (all NEC members) has changed over time, but the members have always been hard-working, gifted, interesting and dedicated men and women.

Change continues at an increasing pace in the WEA. This can be extremely unsettling. It seemed to me in 1995 that the Association needed something to help members understand the changes in the WEA, the reasons for these, and to learn about our history, current provision and possibilities in the future. In my travels around districts I realised that some people were very aware of the WEA, past and present, while others were surprisingly unaware.

In 1996, it was decided that we would develop another Education Committee initiative, the Voluntary Member Training Initiative (VMTI). The main purpose of this undertaking was to develop material which could be used to inform and train voluntary members, and get information from them to inform our work. The Initiative has flourished.

We have put on sessions, some small, some large, all over the country. We have learnt an enormous amount about the WEA in doing this. Our work has been well received. The second edition of our manual, revised, renewed and extended, is ready for publication now. VMTI has taught me a great deal about the WEA and its members. It has given me some very good friends. I know that all I have learnt has been most useful to me in my work as a national officer.

It may not be obvious in this ramble, but I have always been very interested in women's education. I worked on promoting equal opportunities for girls in school, and have been involved in promoting equal opportunities throughout my adult life. I consider that the valuable work of the Women's Education Committee, a committee that works to the Education Committee, has helped to develop this climate within the WEA. We now have some excellent women's education programmes.

In May of next year, I am retiring from WEA national activities. I will be sorry, but I am getting rather old. It is time for others to get their chance. But I will keep on Bellingham branch. After all, who else would?

Acknowledgements & the Future

Colleagues in WEA districts and branches across the Association have made this project possible by writing their stories and passing on the word. This booklet is only a small selection of the wealth of accounts that we have received. They will all be deposited eventually in the national WEA archive at London Metropolitan University. Accounts are still arriving and we are very happy to receive *your* stories. The WEA Women's History Project can be contacted at:

WEA, Unit 22, Shelton Enterprise Centre. Bedford Street, Stoke on Trent, ST1 4PZ.
Tel. 01782 272445. E mail stoke.wea@virgin.net.
and
WEA Women's Education office, Aizlewood's Mill, Nursery Street, Sheffield S3 8GG.
Tel. 0114 2823272. E.mail cscarlett@wea.org.uk

The project has been supported by the WEA Women's Education Committee and the co-ordinating group has consisted of Zoë Munby, Nickie Reed, Chris Scarlett and Annie Winner. This booklet has benefited from the advice and support of a readers' group consisting of Yvon Appleby, Mary Giles, Shirley Harris, Julia Jones, Chris Scarlett and Annie Winner. Alan Allmark, Geraldine D'Arcy, Tracey Holdcroft, Diana and Lionel Munby and Stephen Roberts have proof read and helped with technical issues.

We are grateful to North West district WEA for permission to re-print the accounts by Mary Turner and Hilda Homer from *WEA Voices: a Collection of Students' Writings* and to Luton Branch for permission to re-print an extract from *Canary Girls and Stockpots*.

Thanks to WEA Scotland's *A Century of Learning, 1903-2003*, Heritage Lottery Fund Project, for permission to quote from their interviews.

WEA Women's biographies & autobiographies also received:

Zahida Abbas
Mary Adcock
Evelyn Aldridge
Gill Aldridge
Shirley Allen
Liz Armstrong
Hazel Arnold
Jane Ashcroft
Eileen Aston
Muriel Aydon
Valerie Badger
Doris Bartram
Katherine Bathie
Mina Beaumont
Maureen Belcher
Margaret Bevan
Meiriona Bielawski
Bridget Black
Jean Bould
Amanda Bradshaw
Pam Breden
Wendy Brook
Denise Burness
Marjorie Callow
Dee Cammack
Dickie Cannell
Dell Carr
Doreen Chant
Sue Chant
Vera Chapman
Yvonne Cleave
Stephanie Codd
Barbara Collins
Ann Coman
Alice Cowan
June Cruickshank
Alison Davies
Ida Deodathsingh
Margaret Dugmore
Andree Eaves
Lily Edwards
Mary Edwards
Miss Eustace
Marjorie Evans
Kathy Fauks
Wendy Fenn

Alayne Fenner
Jacqueline Fierek
Deborah Flaherty
Alice Foley
Maureen Ford
Sylvia France
Margaret Frances
Ishbel Fraser
Wilma Fraser
Joy Game
Ally Gardener
Sue Gardener
Janet Garside
Lou Gough
Joan Green
Mary Hall
Fiona Hamilton
Patricia Hare
Ann Harris
Mary Hawkins
Joyce Hayter
Maureen Haywood
Jenny Helson
Angela Hemmings
Maureen Hewitt
Caroline Hill
Elsie Holland
Barbara Holmes
Amanda Hough
Shirley Hughes
Alexina Hutchinson
Irene
Kate James
Jo
Brenda Jobber
Jahanna Jones
Jessie Jones
Rachel Jones
Trisha Joyce
Carol Kalland
Dorothy Kent
M.C.King
Susan Knowles
Trish Land
Marion Last
Sophie Lavender

Ann Lavery
Amanda Law
Miss M.J.P.Lawrence
Gwendolyn M. Lawton
Winnie Leggot
Kate Lodge
Frances Long
Winifred Lovatt
Karen de Lucchi
Gladys Malbon
Lucie Manheim
Andrea Mansell
Jenny Marriot
Janet Marsham
Sheila Mathieson
Ada Mayfield
Ann Millett
Madge Milligan Green
Margaret Milsom
Jessie Millson
Wendy Morgan
Jilly Moysey
Eileen Mumby
Kate Mumby
Kate Munro
Joan Neucount
Sylvia Notarianni
Tina Okara
Pamela
Theresa Peat
Carolyn Perry
Lisa Pickburn
Monica Pink
Frances Pollard
Valerie Portass
Johanna Pratt
Esther Quinn
Barbara Raughton
Sandra Redfern
Nickie Reed
June Richardson
Loretta Rivett
Vi Robinson
Eve Rowley
Elsie Saffin
Patricia Sangster

Irene Saunders
Christine Sharman
Elsie Shaw
Anne Sieve
Kate Singlehurst
Glenys Smith
Andrea Stevens
Maureen Sutton
Ann Sweeney
Cath Sweet
Iris Talbot
Diana Taylor
Karen Taylor
Margaret Taylor
Cynthia Thielker
Ann Thompson
Mary Thompson
Marjorie Thorns
Gladys Titley
Jean Tuzzio
Alice Viggars
Anne Walden
Lynda Walker
Mrs. V. Walker
Margaret Wallis
Betty Warnke
Ann Warrior
Christine Watson
Rosina Watson
Gwyneth Weir
Pauline West
Heidi Whitehouse
Margaret Wilcox
Shirley Wilcox
Muriel Williams
Bett Wilson
Sylvia Wilson-Pranty
Annie Winner
Doreen Winton
Thelma Wolfe
Kathy Wyatt
Jean Wylde
Barbara Young